Frederick Albion Ober

Puerto Rico and its Resources

Frederick Albion Ober

Puerto Rico and its Resources

ISBN/EAN: 9783337379186

Printed in Europe, USA, Canada, Australia, Japan

Cover: Foto ©Suzi / pixelio.de

More available books at **www.hansebooks.com**

PUERTO RICO
AND ITS RESOURCES

BY

FREDERICK A. OBER

Author of Crusoe's Island: A Bird-hunter's Story,
Camps in the Caribbees, Travels in Mexico,
In the Wake of Columbus, A Life of Josephine, Etc.

WITH MAPS AND ILLUSTRATIONS

NEW YORK
D. APPLETON AND COMPANY
1899

PREFACE.

WHILE the writer has always held a preface to be in its very nature a work of supererogation, yet, having told all he knows about Puerto Rico, in this book of facts, he is called upon to write an *ex post facto* introductory. Having exhausted his own stock of information, then, and having presented the gist of what his predecessors in the same field may have garnered, it only remains, perhaps, to tell why he did it, and to mention what had been done before him.

His acquaintance with the island dates from 1880, when he visited every port of importance, and his interest was deepened when, as West-Indian Commissioner for the Columbian Exposition, he revisited its shores. It was not, however, until the present year that opportunity offered for presenting the result of his observations at different times, when the recent war with Spain directed public attention to the subject.

Although Puerto Rico was discovered in 1493, by Columbus, on his second voyage, and settled before the expiration of the sixteenth century's second decade, yet it has not filled an important place in the literature of American voyages and travels. It received casual mention from the early historiographers, as Oviedo, Las Casas, Herrera, and Peter Martyr, in the sixteenth century; from Rochforte in the seventeenth; from Père Labat, Raynal, Jeffreys, and Bryan Edwards, in the eighteenth; and also incidentally, while writing of the voyages of Columbus, the *conquistadores*, and the aborigines, from Navarette, Washington Irving, O'Neil, Reclus, Trumbull, and a few others, in the nineteenth.

The first really valuable work devoted exclusively to the island was published in 1788—the Historia Geografica, Civil y Politica, by Fray Iñigo Abbad y Lasiera—and which has served as the foundation for others since. In 1810, Ledru's Voyage aux Isles d'Teneriffe . . . et Puerto Rico, the portion treating of the latter translated into Spanish in 1863. In 1834 appeared Colonel Flinter's valuable Account of the Present State of the Island; in 1854, the Biblioteca Historica, by a native of and published in the island; in 1873, La Situacion de Puerto Rico, Madrid; in 1878, La Isla de Puerto Rico: Estudio Historico, Geografico y Estadistico, by Manuel Ubeda y Delgada, issued from the insular press; in 1879, Elementos de Geografia de la Isla, a text-book; in 1889, a learned treatise on the aborigines, Los Indios Borinqueños, by Dr. A. Stahl, Puerto Rico; and in 1891, La Isla de Puerto Rico, by J. G. Gomez, Madrid.

Other works of which the author has availed himself in the preparation of this volume are: España, sus Monumentos y Artes, su Naturaleza é Historia: Madrid, 1887; Gran Diccionario Geografico é Historico de España y sus Provincias, Barcelona, 1890; Guia Geografico Militar de España y Provincias Ultramarinas, 1897; Anuario del Comercio, de la Industria (etc.) de España, Cuba, Puerto Rico y Filipinos; the Statesman's Year-Book; the Presupuestos General de Gastos é Ingresos de la Isla de Puerto Rico para 1897–'98; the Trade of Puerto Rico, by F. H. Hitchcock: Washington, 1898; the Hand Book of the American Republics, for 1893, and its Bulletin for August, 1898; and, finally, that invaluable compilation, Military Notes of Puerto Rico, issued by the War Department, Adjutant General's Office, in July of the present year, for the guidance of our military commanders.

Space forbids more than mention of titles, merely, of books to which the writer has been indebted for information; but he would herewith express his sense of obligation to their authors. Moreover, he would tender his grateful acknowledgments to the Library of Congress, and to the heads of the various Governmental departments, particularly the Bureau of Education, the Department of Agriculture, the War and Navy Departments, the Bureau of American Republics, and the Department of State. Their assistance has been of great service, and their courtesy unfailing.

Further, the author feels constrained to add that, in adopting the Spanish orthography, Puerto Rico, instead of the bastard English, "Porto," he has the sanction of highest authority, as, for instance, the United States Board of Geographic Names. The word "Porto" does not occur in any Spanish dictionary, and has not yet became legitimized in English.

WASHINGTON, D. C., *December, 1898.*

CONTENTS.

CHAPTER	PAGE
I.—COMMERCIAL AND STRATEGIC VALUE	1
II.—COASTAL FEATURES, RIVERS, HARBOURS	11
III.—CLIMATE, SEASONS, HURRICANES, ETC.	24
IV.—SOME TROPICAL PRODUCTS	44
V.—SUGAR, TOBACCO, COFFEE, AND CACAO	55
VI.—FRUITS, SPICES, CEREALS, FOOD PLANTS	69
VII.—DYES, DRUGS, WOODS, AND MINERALS	86
VIII.—NATURAL HISTORY, GAME, INSECT PESTS	104
IX.—SAN JUAN, THE CAPITAL	116
X.—CITIES AND TOWNS OF THE COAST	126
XI.—INLAND TOWNS—ROUTES OF TRAVEL	139
XII.—GOVERNMENT AND PEOPLE	158
XIII.—FOODS, DRINKS, DIVERSIONS, ETC.	177
XIV.—THE INDIANS OF PUERTO RICO	198
XV.—A CHAPTER OF HISTORY	208
XVI.—AN AMERICAN POSSESSION	223
APPENDIX	243
INDEX	277

LIST OF ILLUSTRATIONS.

	FACING PAGE
A street in San Juan	*Frontispiece*
Inner harbour, San Juan	8
San Juan Harbour. View from Casa Blanca, Ponce de Leon's house	21
A palm-tree bohio	51
In the cane-field	56
Planter's house, ceiba tree, and royal palms	64
A pineapple field	74
The bread-fruit	94
Edible crabs on sale	106
Ancient and modern sentry boxes, San Juan	117
Church of Santo Domingo, San Juan	123
A tienda, or small shop	128
Native hut, country district	153
A shelter of palm leaves	167
Game cocks on the sidewalk, San Juan	180
Cacao tree and fruit	195
The sea grape	205
A calabash tree	218
Gathering cocoanuts	234
MAP OF PUERTO RICO	282

PUERTO RICO.

I.

COMMERCIAL AND STRATEGIC VALUE.

A NOTEWORTHY event in the history of the United States as a nation is the almost simultaneous acquisition, or practical control, of such tropical islands as Cuba, Puerto Rico, and the Hawaiian group. It is notable, not alone as indicating a departure from ancestral traditions, but as showing that the people of the United States are alive to the needs of the future; for, without an exception, these islands produce naturally all the articles so essential in our domestic economy, raised in tropical countries, in which our own continental territory is deficient.

Although we have a restricted area capable of producing sugar-cane, yet we expend abroad for sugar about one hundred million dollars annually; we have no soil and climate favourable for coffee within the confines of the United States, yet we send to foreign parts another hundred million; and, without going into detail, it may be stated that we expend abroad annually at least two hundred and fifty million dollars for purely tropical products which we can not raise ourselves. Though we could, " at a pinch," find substitutes for coffee and spices in home products, and obtain a limited amount of sugar from beets and sorghum, yet the annual outflow of a quarter billion dollars for such luxuries has gone on just the same.

In a word, the acquisition of these islands, it is believed, will enable us eventually to supply all our wants, as to tropical products which we have hitherto lacked. And, what is more, while they produce the things we lack and need, the people of those islands manufacture next to nothing, and will look to us for all their machinery, flour, cotton and woollen goods—in fact, for everything necessary to civilized communities. While England is talking about an " open door " in the Orient for her commerce and the expansion of trade, we have, though almost fortuitously, opened a door (through the valour of our soldiers and seamen) which will ultimately lead to the commercial conquest of those forty million people south of us, in the West Indies and South America, and the consequent enrichment of millions of our own.

Of these newly acquired tropical possessions of ours, Puerto Rico is the southernmost and also the easternmost. In fact, it lies farther to the east than any portion of Maine, even, and in about the longitude of St. John, New Brunswick; and while the Hawaiian group lies between latitude 19° and 22° north, and Cuba just south of the Tropic of Cancer, Puerto Rico lies between 17° and 18° north, and its northern coast line is one hundred miles to the south of Cuba's southern shores. Within a little more than a thousand miles of the equator, its southern coast facing the Caribbean Sea, its northern toward the Atlantic, it forms the keystone of that arch of islands, the Antillean Archipelago, extending from near the mouth of the Orinoco on the north coast of South America, northward and then westward toward the eastern coast of Honduras, inclosing that vast body of water known as the "Mediterranean of America."

It is about a thousand miles distant from Havana and Key West, twelve hundred from the Isthmus of Panama, fourteen hundred from Nicaragua, fifteen hundred from New York, and three thousand from Cadiz in Spain. These figures, in conjunction with the preceding paragraph, tell another story to the initiated; and that is, its great value, not only as a commercial, but as a strategic centre, or base, in case of future military and naval operations in the Caribbean Sea.

"The trouble with us," a certain senator once said, is that "we are afraid of being great!" It seems at last that we have bravely overcome that dread of territorial expansion, and are no longer afraid of trying, at least, an experiment along that line. The acquisition of Puerto Rico will be in the nature of an experiment on the face of it, but in reality we have been preparing for just such a contingency for many years past. It has long been foreseen by our naval strategists, that if we ever possessed a navy we must also own or control naval bases, or coaling stations, in various parts of the world. By glancing at a map of the world we shall see that Great Britain has girdled the globe with such stations, for the supply and refreshment of her fleets. It was sufficiently emphasized in the East, when our fleet was ordered out of Hong Kong; in the West, when the coal-heaps of St. Thomas and Martinique were declared neutral property. We were for a time wanderers on the face of the seas, with no friendly harbour open to us, no port to welcome us with its shelter.

Fortunately, brave Dewey captured a coaling station at Cavité; in the West Indies we were rendered temporarily independent by colliers accompanying the fleet, and finally by the taking of Guantanamo. But if Dewey had not taken Manila, and if Cervera's fleet had been as strong as was at first reported and we believed, the coaling problem would have been an important factor in determining the success or failure of our plans.

No arguments are needed now to convince our people of the actual necessity for bases of supply at a distance from our continental coast line; but it may surprise many to learn that such acquisitions have been urged for many years, at least thirty past, in the halls of Congress. Away back during Lincoln's administration Secretary Seward had in mind the purchase of the Danish islands of St. Thomas, St. John, and Santa Cruz, and later negotiated a treaty by which, for seven and a half million dollars, we were to acquire them. But for the unexpected opposition of certain senators, when the treaty was up for ratification, we should have bought them; and, notwithstanding the enormous sum we promised to pay for them, though St. John is a fine island, fertile and picturesque, and Santa Cruz covered with rich sugar plantations, yet the sole object in view was the single harbour of St. Thomas!

Even though that harbour has often been visited by hurricanes, and though the island itself is comparatively unproductive, yet our naval experts looked upon its acquisition as a wise measure of diplomacy; but, until quite recently, that harbour, with its dependent island and population, was the only one in the West Indies available, for there was none other for sale. The rapid developments of the war with Spain, however, and the extension of the scheme of conquest to include the island of Puerto Rico, suddenly made us aware of a possible possession, of which we could not have availed ourselves by peaceful means; for Spain would not have sold it at any price.

Here, then, is an island, ours merely at the cost of conquest, which combines all the advantages possessed by St. Thomas in a marked degree, for it has at least six good harbours and a vast extent of fertile territory, as against the one harbour of the Danish isle and its cluster of barren rocks. Strategically, then, as possessing a commanding situation in the Caribbean, with numerous excellent harbours for the asesmbling and refitting of our fleets, with unlimited supply of naval stores, water, fruits, and vegetables, Puerto Rico is of surpassing importance.

Let us glance at those natural features of the island which make it not only a valuable property for us as a national entity, but a potentially lucrative investment individually. In the first place, Puerto Rico is five degrees south of the northern tropic, and so is capable of yielding any variety of plant, fruit, or vegetable that the most favoured region of equatorial America can produce. In the second place, its physical configuration is such that it is generally exempt from the diseases and drawbacks to which most tropic and subtropic countries are subject. In other words, it is a habitable country for the Anglo-Saxon, which can not always be said of regions under or near the equator. This is owing to the fact that the island is hilly, mountainous, and with few swampy sections.

The central backbone of the island is a mountain chain, or cordillera, which reaches its greatest altitude, of some three thousand seven hundred feet, in the peak of the Luquillo Sierra, called El Yunque, a picturesque mountain visible many miles at sea. The chain rises near the Cabeza de San Juan, at the extreme northeastern point of the island, and extends throughout the interior, toward the southwest, which is a heaved-up area of mountains, hills, spurs, valleys, from which run down the many streams and rivers of the island, estimated at thirteen hundred in number, and some of them sixty miles in length.

The length of the island is variously given as from ninety-five to one hundred and five miles, and its breadth from thirty to forty; but probably a safe estimate would make it about one hundred miles in length and thirty-five in average breadth, with a total area of about three thousand six hundred square miles. But though the greater portion is hilly, even mountainous, yet the elevations are generally of such a character, with gently sloping sides and rounded summits, that they are susceptible of cultivation to their very tops. No more beautiful picture can be imagined than the aspect of this island as it is approached from the sea, with the ranges of hills rolling like billows from coast to mountain-tops, which latter are mostly forest-clad; and thus every tint of vegetation is seen, from the lightest to the deepest shade of green.

To revert to the features which make the island valuable as a naval station: Although most of the streams descending from the mountains flow northwardly, yet very few have open or navigable harbours at their mouths, and most of the good seaports are on the southern shore. The north coast boasts one important harbour, however, to which events of the war have called attention, in the famous port of San Juan, the capital and only fortified city on the island. It is an inlet of the northern

Inner harbour, San Juan.

coast, about one third the distance, or thirty-five miles, from Cape San Juan, in the east, to Cape Peña Aguda, in the extreme west. The width of the navigable channel at its mouth is about four hundred yards, and when the water is smooth, vessels carrying five fathoms can cross the bar in safety and run in as far as the wharves near the arsenal. But vessels with the average draft of our battle-ships, or say twenty-four feet, have to exercise great caution in entering, and at all times have to pass within biscuit-throw of the powerful batteries and fortifications on the eastern side.

When a storm is raging or a norther blowing, the harbour mouth, or *boca*, is a sheet of tossing, seething billows, through which the most experienced pilot can only navigate at extreme risk of losing his vessel. Inside, though exposed to the northers, is a deep and beautiful harbour, which can doubtless be improved by dredging and the building of breakwaters, so as to be safe even in the hurricane season.

Arecibo, thirty-five miles west of San Juan, is a place of importance, but has no good harbour; only an open roadstead, in which vessels lie while their cargoes are being transferred by lighters to the shore. Rounding the northwest cape, a magnificent bay is opened, that of Aguadilla, with water deep enough for a battle-ship, and sheltered from the trade-winds, but with no good wharves. The same may be said of Mayagüez, to the south, on the west coast. On the south coast, going east, the first fine harbour is Guanica, where General Miles landed his forces, with water enough for all large vessels; then the harbour of Ponce, with one channel carrying five fathoms; still farther east the small ports of Salinas and Arroyo; and on the eastern end of the island the ports of Humacao, Naguabo, and Fajardo, exposed to the "trades," and with no great depth of water. Thus it may be seen that there are harbours enough and to spare, to suit all seasons and all kinds of weather.

II.

COASTAL FEATURES, RIVERS, HARBOURS.

PUERTO RICO, except for the prolongation of its northeastern end, is almost a parallelogram in coastal outline; east to west, north to south, its coast lines run, as though projected by compass. Seafaring men hail its landfall with delight, and greet the apparition of gigantic Yunque, visible fifty miles at sea, with joy, having in mind the pleasures here of "a turn ashore."

Writing of the extreme regularity of its outline, the eminent geographer, M. Élisée Reclus, says: "Even the islands and islets scattered along the east side seem to form a half-raised extension of the geometrical insular mass. . . . Mona Island, also, off the west coast, in the passage separating Puerto Rico from Santo Domingo, stands on the same submarine bank as the large island of which it is a political dependency. Thus the parting line between the Atlantic and the Caribbean Sea is continued west and east of Puerto Rico in such a way as to connect this island on the one side with Santo Domingo and on the other with the Virgin Islands. But northward and southward the submarine slopes fall regularly to depths of from one thousand to two thousand fathoms, and on the side of the ocean to even five miles."

While Puerto Rico is surpassed by other islands of the Antilles in the altitude of its mountains, still there are several besides the Yunque over three thousand feet in height, as Guilarte in Adjuntas, La Somanta in Aybonito, and Las Tetas de Cerro Gordo in San German, all of which have coffee plantations on their slopes, and are easily ascended on foot or on horseback. There will, doubtless, be some delightful experiences in mountain climbing after we have secured and pacified Cuba and Puerto Rico. The Blue Mountains of Jamaica are glorious and famous, but Luquillo and Tarquino, it is believed, will eclipse them all in the beauties they will reveal. Caves abounding in stalactites, springs of hot and chalybeate water, and streams containing rare fish, are said to be hidden within the mountain valleys of both islands.

Though few of the rivers are navigable for any distance above their mouths, yet not many countries of Puerto Rico's extent are watered by so many streams.

COASTAL FEATURES, RIVERS, HARBOURS. 13

Seventeen rivers, taking their rise in the mountains, cross the valleys of the north coast and empty into the sea. Some of these are navigable two or three leagues from their mouths for schooners and small coasting vessels. Those of Manatí, Loisa, Trabajo, and Arecibo are very deep and broad, and it is difficult to imagine how such large bodies of water can be collected in so short a course. Owing to the heavy surf which continually breaks on the north coast, these rivers have bars across their embouchures which do not allow large vessels to enter. The rivers of Bayamo and Rio Piedras flow into the harbour of the capital, and are also navigable for boats. At high water small brigs may enter the river of Arecibo with perfect safety and discharge their cargoes, notwithstanding the bar which crosses its mouth.

The rivers of the north coast have a decided advantage over those of the south coast, where the climate is drier and the rains less frequent. Nevertheless, the south, west, and east coasts are well supplied with water; and, although in some seasons it does not rain for ten and sometimes twelve months on the south coast, the rivers are never entirely dried up.

From the Cabeza de San Juan, which is the northeast extremity of the island, to the cape of Mala Pascua, which lies to the southeast, nine rivers fall into the sea.

From Cape Mala Pascua to Point Aguila, which forms the southwest angle of the island, sixteen rivers discharge their waters on the south coast.

On the west coast three rivers, five rivulets, and several fresh-water lakes communicate with the sea. In the small extent of three hundred and thirty leagues of area there are forty-six rivers, besides a countless number of rivulets and branches of navigable water.

The rivers of the north coast are stocked with delicious fish, some of them large enough to weigh two quintals.

From the river of Arecibo to that of Manatí, a distance of five leagues, a fresh-water lagoon, perfectly navigable for small vessels through the whole of its extent, runs parallel to the sea at about a mile from the shore.

In the fertile valley of Añasco, on the western coast, there is a canal formed by nature, deep and navigable. None of the rivers are of real military importance; for, though considering the shortness of their course, they attain quite a volume, still it is not sufficient for good-sized vessels.

The rivers emptying on the north coast are Loisa, Aguas Prietas, Arecibo, Bayamón, Camuy, Cedros, Grande, Guajataca de la Tuna, Lesayas, Luquillo, Manatí, Rio Piedras, Sabana, San Martín, Sibuco, Toa, and Vega.

Those emptying on the east coast are Candelero, Dagua, Fajardo, Guayanes, Majogua, and Maonabo.

On the south coast: Aguamanil, Caballon,

COASTAL FEATURES, RIVERS, HARBOURS. 15

Caña, Coamo, Descalabrado, Guanica, Guayama, Guayanilla, Jacagua, Manglar, Peñuela, Ponce, and Vigia.

On the west coast: Aguada, Boquerón, Cajas, Culebrina, Chico, Guanajibo, Mayagüez, and Rincón.

The limits of the Loisa River are: On the east, the sierra of Luquillo (situated near the northeast corner of the island); on the south, the sierra of Cayey, and on the west, ramifications of the latter. It rises in the northern slopes of the sierra of Cayey, and, running in a northwest direction for the first half of its course and turning to northeast in the second half, it arrives at Loisa, a port on the northern coast, where it discharges its waters into the Atlantic. During the first part of its course it is known by the name of Cayagua.

The Sabana River has, to the east and south, the western and southern limits of the preceding river, and on the west the Sierra Grande, or De Barros, which is situated in the centre of the general divide or watershed. It rises in the sierra of Cayey, and, with the name of Piñones River, it flows northwest, passing through Aibonito, Toa Alta, Toa Baja, and Dorado, where it discharges into the Atlantic to the west of the preceding river.

The Manatí River is bounded on the east and south by the Sierra Grande and on the west by the Siales ridge. It rises in the Sierra Grande, and, parallel with the preceding river, it flows through

Siales and Manatí, to the north of which latter town it empties into the Atlantic.

The Arecibo River is bounded on the east by the Siales Mountain ridge, on the south by the western extremity of the Sierra Grande, and on the west by the Lares ridge. It rises in the general divide, near Adjuntas, and flows north through the town of Arecibo to the Atlantic, shortly before emptying into which it receives the Tanama River from the left, which proceeds from the Lares Mountains.

The Añasco River is formed by the Lares Mountain ridge that rises in the eastern extremity of the mountains called Tetas de Cerro Gordo, flowing first northwest, and then west, through the town of its name and thence to the sea.

The Guanajivo River has to its north the ramification of the Lares ridge, to the east the Tetas de Cerro Gordo Mountains, and on the south Torre Hill. In the interior of its basin is the mountain called Cerro Montuoso, which separates its waters from those of its affluent from the right, the Rosario River. It rises in the general divide, flowing from east to west to Nuestra Señora de Montserrat, where it receives the affluent mentioned, the two together then emptying south of Port Mayagüez.

The Coamo River is bounded on the west and north by the Sierra Grande, and on the east by the Coamo ridge. It rises in the former of these sierras, and flowing from north to south it empties east of Coamo Point, after having watered the town of its name.

The Salinas River is bounded on the west by the Coamo ridge, on the north by the general divide, and on the east by the Cayey ridge. It rises in the southern slopes of the Sierra Grande, and flowing from north to south through Salinas de Coamo, empties into the sea.

The northern coast extends in an almost straight line from east to west, and is high and rugged. The only harbours it has are: San Juan de Puerto Rico, partly surrounded by mangrove swamps and protected by the Cabras and the Cabritas Islands and some very dangerous banks; the anchoring ground of Arecibo, somewhat unprotected; and the coves of Cangrejos and Condado. During the months of November, December, and January, when the wind blows with violence from the east and northeast, the anchorage is dangerous in all the bays and harbours of this coast, except in the port of San Juan. Vessels are often obliged to put to sea on the menacing aspect of the heavens at this season, to avoid being driven on shore by the heavy squalls and the rolling waves of a boisterous sea, which propel them to destruction. During the remaining months the ports on this coast are safe and commodious, unless when visited by a hurricane, against whose fury no port can offer a shelter, nor any vessel be secure. The excellent port of San Juan is perfectly sheltered from the effects of the north wind. The hill, upon which the town of that name and the fortifications which defend it are built, protects the vessels anchored in the harbour. The entrance of this port is narrow, and requires a pilot; for the canal which leads to the anchorage, although deep enough for vessels of any dimensions, is very narrow, which exposes them to run aground. This port is several miles in extent, and has the advantage of having deep canals to the east, among a wood of mangrove trees, where vessels are perfectly secure during the hurricane months. Vessels of two hundred and fifty tons can at present unload and take in their cargoes at the wharf. Harbour improvements have been recently made here.

On the northwest and west are the coves of Aguadilla, and the small coves of Rincón, Añasco, and Mayagüez, the latter being protected and of sufficient depth to anchor vessels of moderate draft; the harbour of Real de Cabo Rojo, nearly round, and entered by a narrow channel; and the cove of Boquerón. The spacious bay of Aguadilla is formed by Cape Borrigua and Cape San Francisco. When the north-northwest and southwest winds prevail it is not a safe anchorage for ships. A heavy surf rolling on the shore obliges vessels to seek safety by putting to sea on the appearance of a north wind. Mayagüez Bay is also an open roadstead formed by two projecting capes. It has good anchorage for vessels of a large size, and is well sheltered from the north winds. The port of Cabo Rojo has also good anchorage. Its

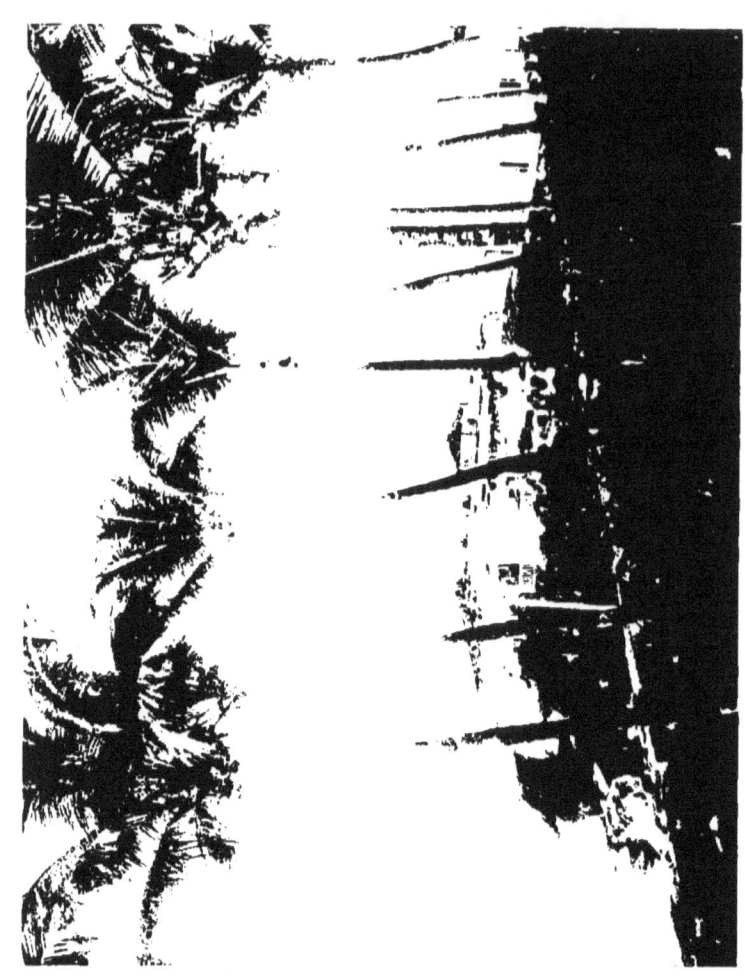

San Juan Harbour. View from Casa Blanca, Ponce de Leon's house.

shape is nearly circular, and it extends from east to west three to four miles. At the entrance it has three fathoms of water, and sixteen feet in the middle of the harbour. The entrance is a narrow canal.

The south coast abounds in bays and harbours, but is covered with mangroves and reefs, the only harbours where vessels of regular draft can enter being Guanica and Ponce. The former of these is the westernmost harbour on the southern coast, being at the same time the best, though the least visited, owing to the swamps and low tracts difficult to cross leading from it to the interior. The nearest towns—San German, Sabana Grande, and Yauco—carry on a small trade through this port.

In the port of Guanica, vessels drawing twenty-one feet of water may enter with perfect safety. Its entrance is about one hundred yards wide, and it forms a spacious basin, completely landlocked. The vessels may anchor close to the shore. It has, in the whole extent, from six fathoms and a half to three fathoms, the latter depth being found in the exterior of the port. The entrance is commanded by two small hills on either side, which if mounted with a few pieces of artillery would defy a squadron to force it. This port would be of immense advantage in time of war. The national vessels and coasters would thus have a secure retreat from an enemy's cruiser on the south coast. Coamo Cove, Aguirre, and

Guayama are also harbours, and the port of Jovos, near Guayama, is a haven of considerable importance. However, it is difficult to enter this port from June to November, as the sea breaks with violence at the entrance, on account of the southerly winds which reign at that season. It has every convenience of situation and locality for forming docks for the repair of shipping. The large bay of Añasco, on the south coast, affords anchorage to vessels of all sizes. It is also safe from the north winds.

Although on the eastern coast there are many places for vessels to anchor, yet none of them are exempt from danger during the north winds except Fajardo, where a safe anchorage is to be found to leeward of two little islands close to the bay, where vessels are completely sheltered. The island of Vieques has also several commodious ports and harbours, where vessels of the largest size may ride at anchor.

Navigation is very active, but the inhabitants do not incline to a seafaring life. The eastern part of the island offers less advantage to commerce than the western, being to the windward and affording less shelter to vessels.

Adjacent to Puerto Rico on the east are the islands of Culebra, Vieques, Santa Cruz, and the group called the Virgin Islands, belonging to England and Denmark; on the west are those of Saona and Mona. The most important of these is Vieques, situated thirteen miles east of Puerto Rico.

COASTAL FEATURES, RIVERS, HARBOURS. 21

It is twenty-one miles long and six miles wide, and is divided for its entire length by a chain of mountains. Its land is very fertile and adapted to the cultivation of almost all the fruits and vegetables that grow in the West Indies. Cattle are raised and sugar cultivated. The mountains are covered with timber forests. It has a population of some six thousand. The town, Isabel Segunda, is on the north, and the port is unsafe in times of northerly winds, like all the anchorages on that side. The few ports on the south are better, the best being Punta Arenas. Not long ago there were two importing and exporting houses on the island of Vieques; but, on account of the long period of drought and the high duties of foreign imported goods, trade has decreased to local consumption only. All supplies are brought from San Juan, the majority being of American origin. The climate is fine and may be considered healthy; there have never been any contagious diseases.

Vieques was temporarily occupied during the two centuries preceding the present by the English and French, but is now entirely under Spanish dominion. Its riches and population are developing from day to day in an admirable manner. Its government under Spanish rule was politico-military, exercised by a colonel. It has a well-built church of masonry at the town of Isabel Segunda.

On the southern coast, opposite the harbour of Ponce, and apparently joined to Puerto Rico by a reef, is the Caja de Muerto Island—" Deadman's Chest "—at which there is a good anchoring ground. Its coasts abound in fish and are surrounded by keys.

To the west of Cape Rojo is the island of Mona, of volcanic origin, with coasts rising perpendicularly to a great height above the sea level. It is inhabited by a few fishermen, and abounds in goats, bulls, and swine in a wild state.

Mona is near the Mayagüez inlet, and gives its name to the broad channels flowing between Puerto Rico and Santo Domingo. Mona, or " Monkey," passage terminates on the west in a bold headland topped by a huge overhanging rock known to seamen by the suggestive name of *"Caigo O No Caigo?"* (Shall I fall or not?)

To the north-northeast of the foregoing and opposite Cape Barrionuevo is Monito Island, a small and elevated rock, inhabited by innumerable waterfowl.

Opposite San Francisco Point is the small island of Deshecho, some two square kilometres in extent and covered with trees of thick foliage.

Fishermen and woodcutters to the number of about five hundred make their home on Culebra, or Snake Island, the second largest in the Passage group, which lies about sixteen miles to the eastward of Cape San Juan. Like Vieques, its coast is indented with many bays, which afford excellent harbours. There are many small hills that are covered with scrub timber, but the soil is so sterile compared with the fertility of Puerto Rico that no attempt is made to cultivate it on an extensive scale, and the inhabitants support themselves by fishing and gathering wood.

III.

CLIMATE, SEASONS, HURRICANES, ETC.

THE climate is hot and moist, yet in the main less injurious to the health of white people than that of adjacent islands. " The heat, rains, and the seasons are, with very trifling variations, the same in all the islands. But the number of mountains and running streams, which are everywhere in view in Puerto Rico, and the general cultivation of the land, may powerfully contribute to purify the atmosphere and render it salubrious to man. The only difference of temperature to be observed throughout the island is due to altitude, a change which is common to every country under the influence of the tropics.

In the mountains the inhabitants enjoy the coolness of spring, while the valleys would be uninhabitable were it not for the daily breeze which blows generally from the northeast and east. For example, in Ponce the noonday sun is felt in all its rigour, while at the village of Adjuntas, four leagues distant in the interior of the mountains, the traveller feels invigorated by the refreshing breezes of a temperate clime. At oné place the thermometer is as high as 90°, while in another it is sometimes under 60°. Although the seasons are not so distinctly marked in this climate as they are in Europe (the trees being always green), yet there is a distinction to be made between them. The division into wet and dry seasons (winter and summer) does not give a proper idea of the seasons in this island; for on the north coast it sometimes rains almost the whole year, while sometimes for twelve or fourteen months not a drop of rain falls on the south coast. However, in the mountains at the south there are daily showers.

As in all tropical countries, the year is divided into two seasons—the dry and the rainy. In general, the rainy season commences in August and ends the last of December, southerly and westerly winds prevailing during this period. The rainfall is excessive, often inundating fields and forming extensive lagoons. The exhalations from these lagoons give rise to a number of diseases, but, nevertheless, Puerto Rico is one of the healthiest islands of the archipelago.

In the month of May the rains commence, not with the fury of a deluge, as in the months of August and September, but heavier than any rain experienced in Europe. Peals of thunder reverberating through the mountains give a warning of their approach, and the sun breaking through the clouds promotes the prolific vegetation of the fields with its vivifying heat. The heat at this season is equal to the summer of Europe, and the nights are cool and pleasant; but the dews are heavy and pernicious to health.

The weather, after a fifteen or twenty days' rain, clears up, and the sun, whose heat has been hitherto moderated by partial clouds and showers of rain, seems, as it were, set in a cloudless sky. The cattle in the pastures look for the shade of the trees, and a perfect calm pervades the whole face of nature from sunrise till between ten and eleven o'clock in the morning, when the sea-breeze sets in. The leaves of the trees seem as if afraid to move, and the sea, without a wave or a ruffle on its vast expanse, appears like an immense mirror. Man partakes in the general languor as well as the vegetable and brute creation.

The nights, although warm, are delightfully clear and serene at this season. Objects may be clearly distinguished at the distance of several hundred yards, so that one may even shoot by moonlight. The months of June and July offer very little variation in the weather or temperature. In August a suffocating heat reigns throughout the day, and at night it is useless to seek for coolness; a faint zephyr is succeeded by a calm of several hours. The atmosphere is heavy and oppressive, and the body, weakened by perspiration, becomes languid; the appetite fails, and the mosquitoes, buzzing about the ears by day and night, perplex and annoy by their stings, while the fevers of the tropics attack Europeans with sudden and irresistible violence. The thermometer frequently exceeds 90°. The clouds exhibit a menacing appearance, portending the approach of the heavy autumnal rains, which pour down like a deluge. About the middle of September it appears as if all the vapours of the ocean had accumulated in one point of the heavens. The rain comes down like an immense quantity of water poured through a sieve; it excludes from the view every surrounding object, and in half an hour the whole surface of the earth becomes an immense sheet of water. The rivers are swollen and overflow their banks, the low lands are completely inundated, and the smallest brooks become deep and rapid torrents.

In the month of October the weather becomes sensibly cooler than during the preceding months, and in November the north and northeast winds generally set in, diffusing an agreeable coolness through the surrounding atmosphere. The body becomes braced and active, and the convalescent feels its genial influence. The north wind is accompanied (with few exceptions) by heavy showers of rain on the north coast; and the sea rolls on that coast with tempestuous violence, while the south coast remains perfectly calm.

When the fury of the north wind abates, it is succeeded by fine weather and a clear sky. Nothing can exceed the climate of Puerto Rico at this season; one can only compare it to the month of May in the delightful province of Andalusia, where the cold of winter and the burning heat of summer are tempered by the cool freshness of spring. This is considered to be the healthiest season of the year, when a stranger may visit the tropics without fear.

The small islands, destitute of wood and high mountains, which have a powerful effect in attracting the clouds, suffer much from drought. It sometimes happens that in Curaçao, St. Bartholomew, and other islands there are whole years without a drop of rain, and after exhausting their cisterns the inhabitants are compelled to import water from the rivers of other islands.

"The land breeze" is an advantage which the large islands derive from the inequality of their surface; for as soon as the sea-breeze dies away, the hot air of the valleys, being rarefied, ascends toward the tops of the mountains, and is there condensed by cold, which makes it specifically heavier than it was before; it then descends back to the valleys on both sides of the ridge. Hence a night wind (blowing on all sides from the land toward the shore) is felt in all the mountainous countries under the torrid zone. On the north shore the wind comes from the south, and on the south shore from the north.

The hurricanes which visit the island, and which obey the general laws of tropical cyclones, are the worst scourges of the country. For hours before the appearance of this terrible phenomenon the sea appears calm; the waves come from a long distance very gently until near the shore, when they suddenly rise as if impelled by a superior force, dashing against the land with extraordinary violence and fearful noise. Together with this sign, the air is noticed to be disturbed, the sun red, and the stars obscured by a vapour which seems to magnify them. A strong odour is perceived in the sea, which is sulphurous in the waters of rivers, and there are sudden changes in the wind. These omens, together with the signs of uneasiness manifested by various animals, foretell the proximity of a hurricane.

This is a sort of whirlwind, accompanied by rain, thunder, and lightning, sometimes by earthquake shocks, and always by the most terrible and devastating circumstances that can possibly combine to ruin a country in a few hours. A clear, serene day is followed by the darkest night; the delightful view offered by woods and prairies is diverted into the dreary waste of a cruel winter; the tallest and most robust cedar trees are uprooted, broken off bodily, and hurled into a heap; roofs, balconies, and windows of houses are carried through the air like dry leaves, and in all directions are seen houses and estates laid waste and thrown into confusion.

The fierce roar of the water and of the trees being destroyed by the winds, the cries and moans of people, the bellowing of cattle and neighing of horses, which are being carried from place to place by the whirlwinds, the torrents of water inundating the fields, and a deluge of fire being let loose in flashes and streaks of lightning, seem to announce the last convulsions of the universe and the death agonies of nature itself.

Sometimes these hurricanes are felt only on the north coast, at others on the south, although generally their influence extends throughout the island.

Earthquakes are somewhat frequent, but not violent or of great consequence. The natives foretell them by noticing clouds settle near the ground for some time in the open places among the mountains. The water of the springs emits a sulphurous odour or leaves a strange taste in the mouth; birds gather in large flocks and fly about, uttering shriller cries than usual; cattle bellow and horses neigh, etc. A few hours beforehand the air becomes calm and dimmed by vapours which arise from the ground, and a few moments before there is a slight breeze, followed at intervals of two or three minutes by a deep rumbling noise, accompanied by a sudden gust of wind, which are the forerunners of the vibration, the latter following immediately. These shocks are sometimes violent and are usually repeated, but, owing to the special construction of the houses, they cause no damage.

As the writer remarked years ago: While we can not marshal the tropical seasons, as we can those of the temperate zones, under their distinctive appellations, and say, This is spring, this is winter, and this is glorious summer, yet there is a well-recognised difference between them. Nature here is a veritable wanton, for, having no real winter to contend with, having no frost, no snow, she has only sun and rain to interfere with as well as to promote vegetable growth and the development of animal life.

As a rule throughout the West Indies, the first three months of the year are decidedly the best for travelling and for out-of-door occupations. The days are hot but endurable, the nights are cool, and storms are infrequent. With April and May gentle showers are ushered in, which stimulate the growth of plants that have been set out in anticipation of these rains. The negro farmer sets out his eddoe, banana, and plantain shoots, and buries in the earth his yams, sweet potatoes, etc., which form the staples of the " provision grounds." Roses bloom the year round, but there is a perceptible increase in blossoms and fragrance; the beautiful frangipanni expands its pink and white whorls upon bare stems, and fills the air with its perfume. About the honey-scented flowers of the palms, limes, and acaciæ, the bees and butterflies cluster in fluttering clouds, while the humming bird darts from tree to flower, his coat of burning mail glowing like a gem.

June is the month for flowers, as in the north,

and it is not unusual to see a whole forest starred with blossoms, as you sail along the coast of some island, at a distance sufficient to mass the tree-tops into one vast sea or plain of verdure. July usually brings an increase of rains, especially in the mountainous islands, and sends the mercury in the thermometer upward a few degrees; but even in this midsummer month the heat is not uncomfortable, and sunstrokes rarely, if ever, occur. July, however, is the month set down in the calendar as that in which the " hurricane season " begins, and from the 25th of this month until the same date in October it is well to be prepared for a " blow."

But August is the recognised month for hurricanes, and deep anxiety is felt; not less in September, as the sun approaches the line and the " equinoctial storm " is due. Still, the hurricane season will not allow itself to be " cribbed, cabined, and confined " within the limits of three short months, and skips along whenever its blithe fancy takes it, having a way of turning up at most unexpected seasons, instances being on record of terrible hurricanes in December, and at least one big storm or tornado as early in the year as the month of March. But as October draws on, the suspense of the West Indians gives place to a feeling of relief, and when the great rains of the autumnal equinox set in all fear subsides, and they give themselves up to the somewhat equivocal enjoyment of a season of torrential rains. The last three months of the year are, as a rule, cooler, and more enjoyable than the others; but in these, also, more endemic fevers are prevalent than in the others.

The life of the West Indian thermometer, it may be mentioned in passing, is as sluggish and uneventful as that of a government clerk. The regularity with which it performs its allotted task is at first surprising to a visitor from the north, as its daily range is scarcely more than ten degrees —say, from 70° in the morning to 80° at noon and 76° at dusk. And even a hurricane partakes of this well-ordered system (except for the occasionally erratic storms that have been mentioned). It rarely fails to come on "schedule time," and is not often unexpected. In fact, after the people of these islands have prepared for it, by hunting some hole or cellar, into which they crawl—with a barometer, a stock of "cane juice" and food for the day or night—if, when they emerge, they do not find the roofs of their dwellings have come off, they are somewhat disappointed. For the hurricane and the earthquake are two things on which they pride themselves, as in a sense peculiar to their insular domains. Earthquakes are the most frequent, it has been observed, in the first three months of the year, so that the inhabitants of these islands have something disquieting on hand pretty much all the time.

The "hurricane season" was recognised as a regular institution many years ago by the Government of the Danish West Indies (St. Thomas, St. John, and Santa Cruz), which appointed the 25th of July as a day of humiliation and prayer and the 25th of October as one of thanksgiving. Observations extending through many years, in St. Thomas, show that during a period of some one hundred and eighty years that island has been visited by devastating hurricanes at least ten times. The hurricane is very erratic in its course, and, while an island lying in its path might be entirely devastated, another not far away might escape without a wreck. Sir R. H. Schomburgk, an eminent British explorer, who spent many years in the West Indies (and who, by the way, discovered the *Victoria Regia*), found recorded, during a period of three hundred and fifty years (from 1492 to 1846), one hundred and twenty-seven hurricanes and destructive gales. Of this number, one occurred in March, four in June, eleven in July, forty in August, twenty-eight in September, and two in December. Thirteen of the number had no date recorded.

Some years are more fateful than others; and perhaps, indeed, there may be cycles of hurricanes which, if we could determine, might be of infinite benefit to commerce and shipping. At all events, the establishment in the West Indies of stations connected with our own Weather Bureau will be of inestimable service to mankind, and perhaps tend to a solution of the mystery.

While Cuba, Jamaica, and Santo Domingo come within the hurricane radius, Puerto Rico and St. Thomas, together with the islands of the Lesser Antilles, suffer much more than the Greater Antilles, as a whole. The natives of these islands had a name for the hurricane, from which the English word is derived—namely, *ouragan*, which has come to us through the Spanish *huracan*. They stood in great fear of these *ouraganes*, and, though they made long voyages in their small canoes or dugouts, they took good care not to venture far at sea during the continuance of the hurricane season.

The logs of vessels visiting the West Indies abound with references to the hurricane, as, for instance, this from a Danish packet:

" Came to anchor in St. Thomas and landed

the mails. Here the hurricane of the 2d instant seems to have concentrated all its force and fury, for the harbour and town were a scene that baffles all description. Thirty-six ships and vessels totally wrecked all around the harbour, among which about a dozen had sunk or capsized at their anchors. Some rode out by cutting away their masts, and upward of one hundred seamen were drowned. The harbour is so choked up with wrecks that it is difficult to pick out a berth for a ship to anchor. . . . The destructive powers of this hurricane will never be forgotten. The fort at the entrance of the harbour is levelled with its foundations, and its twenty-four-pounders thrown about as though it had been battered to pieces by cannon-shot."

St. Thomas has been the object of particular spite, it would seem, on the part of old Æolus, and it was perhaps owing to that destructive hurricane and tidal wave in 1867, when we were negotiating for the acquisition of the island, that our legislators changed their minds and voted against its purchase. At that time hundreds of houses were levelled, and one of our war-ships was swept high and dry ashore, amid the wreckage of warehouses and dwellings.

The West Indians guard as much as possible from the hurricanes by building their houses of stone, in the main, with massive walls, and providing strong bars for doors and windows. When the barometer gives notice of the approach of a storm these bars are brought out and everything is at once made fast. Doors and window-shutters are closed, barred, and double-locked, and the town looks as if it were deserted by all human beings. The state of suspense, while the hurricane rages, is simply awful, for no one knows when the house may fall and bury all beneath its ruins. Add to this the howling of the blasts, the crash of falling trees, the piercing cries for help from wounded and dying, and one may faintly picture the terrible scene. To venture out is almost certain death, the air is so filled with flying missiles, such as boards, branches of trees, tiles, bricks, and stones.

Some hurricanes have passed into history for their destructiveness and attendant loss of human life. From the time of Columbus to the present day, West Indian chronicles are replete with allusions to the dreadful visitations. In the year 1766, for example, the island of Martinique was devastated by a hurricane that destroyed the dwelling of Josephine, the beautiful creole, who subsequently became the wife of Napoleon.

She was then but three years old, but the terrors of that dreadful storm were such that she remembered it all through her eventful life. Josephine's house was levelled to the ground, and her family was forced to take refuge in a cave, an artificial construction called a *case-à-vent*, or hurricane-house.. This is usually built into or under the side of a hill, with walls of stone several feet in thickness, and, as far as possible, in a sheltered situation. The door is of thick plank, there are no windows, and, as may be imagined, the air within, if the storm last long, becomes most oppressive. To such a shelter fled the father of Josephine, and for hours he and his family remained in this living tomb, until the force of the storm was passed, when they emerged to witness the total desolation of their plantation. For ten years thereafter this illustrious woman lived, as a child, in the upper rooms of the old sugar-mill, the walls of which were standing a few years ago.

Twenty-eight French and seven English vessels were wrecked during that storm, besides scores of canoes and small craft. Ninety persons perished under the ruins of their own houses, and twice that number were wounded in the capital, St. Pierre, alone.

In the year 1780, during a hurricane in the southern islands, a French fleet containing sixty merchant vessels and transports with five hundred soldiers was wrecked, only ten vessels escaping.

Two British men-of-war sank in the Mono passage, and it is said that sixteen thousand people perished in Martinique, St. Lucia, and Jamaica. In 1888 the coast of Cuba was swept by a hurricane, and in the town of Sagua la Grande alone one thousand persons perished. In 1846, 1,872 houses were demolished during a hurricane, and 216 vessels sunk.

One of the most destructive hurricanes occurred so recently as 1891, when the island of Martinique was prostrated by a terrible tornado, from the effects of which it may never recover.

Early on the morning of the 18th of August (says the United States consul in his report), the sky presented a leaden appearance, decidedly threatening, with occasional gusts of variable winds, mostly from east-northeast. The temperature was very oppressive during the day. The barometer varied only slightly, but was a little higher than usual until afternoon, when it commenced to fall, at first gradually, then very rapidly. It is stated by fishermen who were in the vicinity of Caravel Rock (in the sea channel) that an immense wave about a hundred feet high passed from the direction of St. Lucia, closely followed by another smaller one, although the sea in the vicinity was quite calm at the time.

The storm struck the east side of the island at about 6 P. M., rushing through the ravines and destroying everything in its path. On the elevated plains the ruin was complete. One very peculiar feature of the hurricane was the deafness experienced by every one during the storm—possibly the result of the reduced barometric pressure. During the cyclone the wind veered from east-northeast to south-southeast, from the latter point being the most destructive; there were incessant flashes of sheet lightning unaccompanied by thunder, and immediately after the storm two distinct shocks of earthquake, at intervals of about five seconds. Early in September following I visited La Trinité and noted that all the way the destruction was most complete, the trees and all vegetation looking as though there had been a forest fire, although without the charred appearance. The sugar-cane suffered least, and the loss, with favourable weather, will not amount to more than one fifth its normal value. The factories and distilleries appear to have been more completely destroyed than any other property. The thermometer ranged from 90° to 100° during the storm, and there was a deluge of rain, one account stating that over four inches fell in a few hours that evening.

My own residence was unroofed and flooded with water, as was the case with nine tenths of the buildings of St. Pierre, and throughout the island. The loss of life was comparatively small in the capital, but large in the interior towns, notably in Morne Rouge (a mountain resort above St. Pierre), where eight in one family alone lost their lives. The total loss of life, so far as reliable information can be obtained, was seven hundred, and the loss of property was enormous. All the fruit, the main reliance of the labouring classes, was destroyed, and prices of provisions at once advanced three hundred per cent. Every vessel along the coast was either wrecked or badly damaged, about fifty sail in all. The scene the island presents would be difficult to describe, and the inhabitants are sorely stricken and demoralized. Such a night of terror the imagination can scarcely picture.

This account, valuable from being an official report by an eye-witness, the writer of this chapter can attest as being authentic and moderate in its description, as he was at the island within four months of the occurrence, and saw the effects of that terrible storm, in the hundreds of unroofed dwellings and the almost total destruction of the shade and forest trees.

During a residence in the West Indies of several years he experienced but two hurricanes, but has no desire to extend his acquaintance with those devastating storms. Once, in the island of Tobago, his camp was destroyed, immense forest trees were thrown to the ground, vast spaces of hillside washed away, and it seemed that no sort of animal life was left. But a few days after the denizens of the forest appeared again, all nature smiled as if no storm had ever occurred, and even the fragile humming birds came fluttering about their accustomed feeding places.

In the island of Puerto Rico hurricanes have been very destructive in times past. One of the earliest chronicled occurred in 1525, and all through its history occur such notes as *un furioso huracan*, etc. In 1678 an English fleet in the harbour of San Juan was almost entirely destroyed by a hurricane just as its commander had summoned the fortress to capitulate. In 1702 a Puerto Rican squadron was totally destroyed in the same harbour as it was on the point of sailing to attack an English fleet. So it would appear as though the harbour of San Juan, despite its almost land-locked character, was not entirely safe from the attacks of the hurricane. That of St. Thomas, sixty miles distant, is equally exposed, though the latter opens to the south, while the former faces north.

The island was also visited by a terrible hurricane in 1772, and in 1825 another destroyed the towns of Patillas, Maunabo, Yabucoa, Gurabo, and Caguas, as well as causing much damage in other towns in the east, north, and central districts of the island.

And yet hurricanes are not so frequent here as in other islands, though they have been destructive in the past and are likely to be in the future.

The extension by the United States Government of its "Weather Bureau service" to the West Indies will enable the Puerto Riqueños to seek a shelter when a hurricane is due; and probably the much-abused "cyclone cellar" of our great West will be among the first blessings of an advanced civilization we shall bestow upon those dwellers in the turbulent tropics!

In fact, on the occasion of the terrible visitation of 1898, but a few weeks after the system was established in the West Indies (and only six weeks after benighted Haiti had refused our Government permission to establish a station at Mole San Nicolas) the warnings it sent out probably saved many lives and much valuable shipping. As it was, hundreds of lives were lost in Barbadoes and St. Vincent, and thousands rendered homeless.

Mean Monthly Temperature at San Juan de Puerto Rico during Five Years' Observation.

Hours of the Day.	Jan.	Feb.	Mar.	April.	May.	June.	July.	Aug.	Sept.	Oct.	Nov.	Dec.
Seven in the morning...	72	72½	74	78	78	82	85	86	80½	77	75	75
Noon.........	82	81	82	83	85	86	90	92	88	85	84	80
Five in the evening...	78	74	78	80	81	84	87	90	83	82	80	79

IV.

SOME TROPICAL PRODUCTS.

WHILE this delectable island has been of great value to Spain, it is likely to be vastly more important to the United States, merely on account, if for no other reason, of its contiguity. Such perishable products as bananas and other fruits of the tropics, green cocoanuts, etc., the raising of which is always profitable, can be brought to our ports on swift steamers and will find a ready sale. In fact, it will not take many years to show the wisdom of annexing this tropical territory to the United States and bringing it under the protecting wing of the American eagle.

It is easy enough to generalize and say this and that may be raised here, and that generous nature brings forth her fruits spontaneously, while indolent man reclines in a hammock and only opens his mouth to let them drop into it. But, while in the main this may be true—that nature is generous—still, since all men are not vegetarians and can not subsist on fruits alone, it will probably be found necessary to work for a living here as elsewhere—that is, if one desires to live well.

And yet perhaps there is no country where man can live with less effort than in this island, and in many similar islands scattered throughout the Caribbean Sea.

In a word, it might be said that the products of Puerto Rico are those of the West Indies in general, and cover the entire range of tropical agriculture and horticulture. Nature has singularly blessed this beautiful island, giving it, in the first place, eminence of location, right in the heart of the Antillean system, between the Atlantic and the Caribbean Sea, making it strategically important as well as endowing it with a delightful climate.

In the second place, its physical configuration is such that, though situated within the tropics, its great mountain range, culminating in Luquillo, renders available the cooler temperature of the temperate zone, by merely a change of altitude. As in Mexico, with its three different zones of climate and vegetation, in Puerto Rico we find the same conditions prevailing. Along the coast is the lowland of the *tierra caliente*, or the hot region; next comes the *tierra templada*, or delightful temperate zone; and lastly, well up the mountain sides, the *tierra fria*, or colder zone.

Not that we find in Puerto Rico, with total area of thirty-six hundred square miles, these climatic zones so vastly displayed or so distinctly defined as in Mexico; but we do have here those physical continental features as modified by insular environment. But, while other islands of the Antilles send mountains farther skyward and possess the same general character of soil, climate, and productions, yet there is none so universally cultivable as Puerto Rico. From sea to mountain top almost, from shore to forest line anyway, the slopes of its thousands hills may be cultivated without interruption. As to its many valleys and rolling plains: their fertility has long been known and appreciated, as evidenced by the investments of foreign as well as domestic capital in the cultivation of the sugar-cane.

In a bird's-eye view of this territory, now within the jurisdiction of the United States, we will begin at the coast and note the prominent productions which are not common in our own country. The cays and islets, like those on the coast of Florida, are frequently bordered with the curious mangrove, perched upon its long, spider-like legs; of no particular use, except as a land-builder, as by means of its adventitious shoots it extends itself in shallow waters, and is thus an advance courier of terrene extension.

SOME TROPICAL PRODUCTS. 47

The mangrove stands with its roots in salt water, filling muddy bays and inlets; but farther back on the shore, yet well within reach of the waves in time of storms, rising sometimes from banks of pure sand, is the cocoa palm, forming a living barrier between the sea and cultivable lands. Broad valleys stretch along the shore, and extend back toward the hills; vast waving billows of sugar-cane, bordered by the ranks of cocoa palms. Though sometimes straying inland, particularly on level plains and valleys with slight elevation, the cocoa palm is usually found growing near the shore. Its range extends northward from the equator twenty-eight degrees; it may be found growing in Florida, but will not flourish above latitude 25° 30′ north. It is an exotic here, though long acclimated, coming probably from Ceylon and the East Indies. Growing always near the salt water, its nuts fall into the waves and are carried to every part of the world, and when cast ashore in climates favourable to their growth, germinate, and produce sturdy trees. The cocoa palm attains a height, when in good condition, of from sixty to eighty feet, lives, it is said, a hundred years, bears a hundred nuts annually, and has a hundred uses for man.

It is essentially a poor man's tree, from which he derives not only drink and sustenance, but material for his dwelling. Huts made of palm logs, thatched with palm leaves or the spathes that overtop the clusters of nuts, are cool, cleanly, cheaply made, and suffice for the needs of probably two thirds of the dwellers in tropic countries. Our soldiers in Cuba have become acquainted with the cooling water contained in the ivory chambers of green cocoanuts, and can testify to its refreshing qualities. Cocoa water is the safest beverage for the morning tipple, as well as for any time of day when one is not overheated. Those who have resided a long time in the tropics, and have become " bibulously inclined," make it their morning " eye-opener " by adding gin or native rum. There is then a negative virtue in those liquors, inasmuch as they will not hurt you so much as when taken raw!

To more particularly enumerate the manifold uses of the palm: The natives extract from its roots a remedy for fevers; boats, houses, and furniture are made from its trunk, the wood having a beautiful grain and being highly esteemed in cabinet work; combs are made from the foot stalks of the leaves, which are used for thatching huts, in making baskets, mats, hats, etc., while the fibrous material at their bases is used for sieves, and also woven into clothing; from the flowers an astringent is obtained used in medicine, and from the

SOME TROPICAL PRODUCTS.   49

flower-stalks palm wine, or "toddy," is derived, which again, in Ceylon, is distilled into arrack, while both sugar and vinegar are products of the natural juice. From the fruit or nut, besides the delicious water and jelly it contains when green, comes the *copra*, or kernel, which is dried and exported, and yields fifty per cent its weight in pure oil, after which the refuse is valuable for manure, as well as for fowl and cattle food. From the husks *coir* is made, which is manufactured into ropes, brooms, brushes, bedding, etc., and the shells themselves are useful as lamps, cups, spoons, and scoops. In fact, one might go on enumerating the various articles used in the primitive domestic economy of the tropical native, and find them all supplied by the cocoa palm.

The cocoanut, as a dried product, is shipped abroad, chiefly to the United States, to the amount of some three million annually; but this is no criterion of its abundance, for millions more are used in the island in the green state, and other millions go to waste. The cocoa palm is readily grown, and though rather slow in coming to maturity, can be made a profitable adjunct to a plantation. It will grow in any soil except clay, even in pure sand. Any one who has seen the oases of the Algerian desert will recall the mounds of verdure topping sterile tracts, composed of the date palms, their roots fed by underground springs; and in similar surroundings, also, the cocoa palm will live and thrive. A nut, a hole in the sand filled with soil, plenty of salt water, and a little care for a few years, are all this palm demands. It will flower about the fifth year, produce nuts from the sixth to the tenth, and thereafter yield a constantly increasing crop for a generation, at least. The better way is to plant the nuts in nurseries and transplant to rows about forty feet apart, or forty odd to the acre, when the plants are six months old. Good healthy nuts must be selected, thoroughly ripened, and planted in trenches about a foot apart, their stalk ends slightly elevated. So essentially is the cocoa the product of a maritime climate that when planted far from the sea a considerable quantity of salt must be put in the holes if fine trees are desired.

All other species of palm grow here, most of them introduced, but some of them native. The most noticeable of native species, is the glorious royal palm, which is indigenous here as well as in Cuba. It dots the fields and stands in groups about the houses, and has commercial as well as æsthetic value, a full grown tree being worth at least ten dollars for its lumber. Most of the native huts are roofed with the great, boat-like spathes of this palm,

A palm-tree bohio.

which are sometimes six feet long and three broad. These huts, by the way, are called *bohios*, to distinguish them from more pretentious houses, framed and tiled, which are known under the generic name of *casas*. The palm spathes, which fall from the tree after the seeds are ripe, are pressed out flat, laid in rows over a framework of poles, and kept in place by other poles tied loosely above them. A palm-tree *bohio* costs nothing more than the labour necessary to make it, assuming the trees to belong to the land on which it is built, and can be erected in a day or two.

Another native palm, found farther up in the hills and mountains, is the beautiful *oreodoxa*, tallest of the tribe, and which sometimes attains a height of one hundred and fifty feet. All the palms, and particularly this oreodoxa, are celebrated for their " cabbage," or terminal bud, which is a delicious morsel when divested of its outer wrappings and boiled like cauliflower or cabbage. Its utilization thus implies, of course, the destruction of the tree; but that is a matter of little consequence to a hungry native with a forest full of palms, and who only considers the labour necessary to cut down the tree, and not the injury he does to the landscape. This vandalism is not confined to the Spanish islands, either, for there was once a planter in the English island of Barbados who, when the question arose as to the height of a magnificent palm on his estate, ordered it cut down, that he might ascertain to a certainty. He wagered that it would measure over one hundred and fifty feet; and he won the wager, but he lost the palm.

Another product of the palm sometimes adorns the native's table, and that is a luscious fat grub of the palm beetle, which is occasionally found burrowing in the heart of the tree. This is roasted and eaten as a *bonne bouche* of great excellence. There are also other palms, as the mountain and *gri-gris*, which are native, while all the foreign varieties, as the sago, date, and areca, are to be found in cultivation. All are useful, and doubtless, with improved methods of cultivation and horticulture, and with the experiments that Yankee proprietors will introduce, they will yield vastly more in the future than they have in the past.

Then there are the bananas, which flourish all over the lowland region and far up the hills. According to the last available statistics, two hundred million bananas are shipped annually from this island, and there are no plants requiring less attention and less time than bananas and plantains. All varieties may be grown here, and there is no reason why Puerto Rico, under American protection and with the stimulus of American enterprise, shall not rival Jamaica in its production of these delicious fruits. One planting of a banana shoot will last for years, as it practically renews itself, and after the second year the owner of a banana plantation has only to pick and ship the fruit, and await the returns in cash.

Little capital is needed for a start in banana culture; it is the poor man's crop, only provided he can obtain a small side-hill farm, a few banana shoots, and supply himself with a stock of patience to last a couple of years. While the banana and its sister plantain grow best in rich and level lands, yet they can be cultivated on hillsides so steep that no plough can furrow them, and where it would be impossible to raise sugar-cane with profit. The plantain is in many respects more desirable as a table supply than the banana, as it is better cooked than raw, and furnishes a staple food of which one does not so soon tire as an article of diet.

These twin sisters of the tropical world are among its most glorious productions, and, according to Humboldt, will yield vastly more to the acre than almost anything else that grows. He estimated that the same space of ground necessary to produce thirty-three pounds of wheat and ninety-eight of potatoes would yield four thousand pounds of bananas; and as to its nutriment, it is superior to wheat as well as meat, pound for pound.

The parent plant sends up a number of side shoots or suckers, from which others are propagated. When these shoots are about two feet in height they are cut off by a spade or cutlass (*machéte*) and set out in rows in soil well worked, about fifteen feet apart each way, or about one hundred and sixty plants to the acre. The land should be well drained and weeded, and a crop will be in evidence a year from planting, and thenceforth fruit will be maturing all the time.

V.
SUGAR, TOBACCO, COFFEE, AND CACAO.

THE vegetable kingdom is rich enough in plants, native and introduced, which grow perfectly well in a tropical climate, without going far afield for other cultivations. The main products of the lowlands, sugar and tobacco, require such skill, capital, and attention that a novice would very likely fail if he were to attempt their cultivation, let alone the probable impossibility of obtaining the necessary lands; for Puerto Rico is not a wild country sparsely populated, but has a rather dense population of more than eight hundred thousand, which at present occupies, if it does not utilize, the greater portion of its thirty-six hundred square miles of area. The methods of cultivation, so far as sugar is concerned, are those in vogue in Cuba; but there are fewer great *ingenios*, with perfect appliances for crystallizing and refining, and more of the *trapiche de buey*, or one-ox mills, here. Still, the annual export of sugar rises to seventy thousand tons, with great opportunity, in the near future, for expansion of territory cultivated and of output.

We can not overlook these two great staples, sugar and tobacco, as they rank respectively second and third in the island's products. Sugar is at its best in the littoral region, requires a tropical climate, hot and moist, and prefers a saline atmosphere. It grows in almost any soil, but in the rich volcanic loams of the Lesser Antilles does better than anywhere else outside of Cuba. It is propagated by cuttings, which consist of the two or three upper joints of the cane, and these are placed in furrows made by the plough or in holes ten or twelve inches deep and four or five feet apart. Two cuttings, each about six inches long, are placed in every hole, with but an inch protruding above the ground, and these will grow into a " bunch " of canes which, in fertile soil, will yield four gallons of juice, from which four pounds of muscovado sugar may be obtained. The best time for planting is from October to January, according to the season, whether wet or dry; affected, of course, by local conditions. The land should be well cultivated and mellow, and the weeds removed until the cane is high enough to shade the soil. On very fertile soils, however, it is not necessary to plant oftener than once in ten or fifteen years, as the roots of the cane left in the ground after cutting send up *rattoons*, or shoots—in other words, replant themselves. Though some

In the cane-field.

deep volcanic soils will thus reproduce the original cane for fifteen or twenty years, it is not considered good farming to allow this process to go beyond four or five.

The universal cropping time in the West Indies is during the first four or five months of the year, or from January to May, inclusive. Then the air is redolent of sweet odours, and the negroes and cattle on the plantations are fat and sleek from the unlimited devouring of crude cane and sugar. The sugar-cane was introduced here early in the sixteenth century, probably from the Canaries, via Santo Domingo, and found a congenial home, as well as in Cuba. It is doubtful if it ever grew to such proportions in its native home as in the West Indies, where specimens of cane have been raised over twenty feet in height, though the average height in the field is from eight to ten feet. The canes are cut off close to the ground and then chopped into lengths of four or five feet, tied up in bundles, and carted to the mill, which may be a *trapiche de buey*, or bullock-mill; a small affair run by water power; or an immense *ingenio*, run by steam, with electric lights and motors, and all the latest inventions for clarifying, crystallizing, and refining the juice. The simplest processes, however, have hitherto prevailed in Puerto Rico, and it is in the establishment of great central factories—practically refineries—called by the French *usines*, that American capital may find a profitable venture. It is almost as impracticable for the average planter to refine his own sugar as for the average farmer in the temperate zone to grind his own wheat into flour. In the ordinary "sugar works" the latest scientific methods are not utilized, and most of them are run in as primitive a manner as in the old-time "slavery days," when black men were so plentiful that it was cheaper to "buy than to breed," and manual labour took the place of steam and electricity. When the railroad system of Puerto Rico is completed, and all the chief settlements connected it will be an easy matter to erect a few immense *usines* in centrally located valleys, with tramways radiating in various directions and communication by land and water with the hundreds of small plantations, by which means the small proprietors may bring their products to the central factories. At the same time, the fact should not be lost sight of that of late years sugar has not been a profitable cultivation, except on a vast scale, owing to various causes, such as lack of cheap labour, since the abolition of slavery, and the increasing cultivation of the sugar beet.

There is, of course, no region like the famous "Vuelta Abajo" of Cuba for the raising of high-grade tobacco, but the "weed" of Puerto Rico is said to press it close in competition. Indeed, there is no reason why it should not, for the peculiar soil of the Abajo—a light, sandy loam, rich in lime, potash, and vegetable humus—is found in this island in many valleys, and the climatic conditions are similar and favourable. And as most of the tobacco raised here, to the amount of more than half a million dollars annually, has hitherto been sent to Cuba, one should be pardoned a suspicion that Puerto Rico's product may be found incorporated in not a few of those "genuine Havanas" for which the gilded youth of our country pay such fabulous prices!

But tobacco is *caprichoso* (capricious), the Spaniards say, and the right combination of soil and climate can be found only by experimentation. It was first discovered by Columbus in the Bahamas, but receives its name from an island—Tobago—farther south of Puerto Rico than the latter is of Cuba, and hence much nearer. A native of the tropics, then, although it will grow in northern climes, yet the heat and humidity necessary for its perfect development are said to exist only in such regions as the West Indies. Puerto Rico has grown tobacco for many years, and produces a fairly good brand of cigars, which ranks with those of Vera Cruz in Mexico. But the art of curing the *cohiba*, as the tobacco plant is called, has never been acquired by the Puerto-Riqueños. Now that many of the Cuban " fabricators " have found a home in the island, it will not be long before it will be exporting " Reinas de Puerto-rico," " Conchas de San Juan," " Partagas de la Borinquen," etc. The smokers of the United States alone are said to consume some two hundred million so-called " Havanas," but it is well known that not more than fifty million real Havanas are annually exported to this country, so it is clear that a few of our four billion cigars yearly sent up in smoke are not the genuine article. In fact, it is extremely difficult, and always was, to find good Havana cigars in the capital of Cuba itself, for the best are absorbed, at fabulous prices, by the *ricos hombres* of European courts.

It will not be difficult to gain a prestige for the Puerto Rico tobacco like that enjoyed by the Cuban, if planters with brains and capital will secure control of some vast valley, plant it with genuine Cuban seed, and establish a name for its products. Next to the right soil and climate—which exist in this island—the most important factor in producing a perfect article is great care in raising the plant and curing the leaves. It is only necessary to overcome the native indolence to secure good results; and as tobacco, unlike sugar, is always in demand at a good price, and its cultivation is easy, it would seem to open a profitable perspective for American capital.

According to the *Estadistica General del Comercio Exterior* of 1897, Puerto Rico exported to the amount of $646,556 in tobacco, $3,747,891 in sugar, and $8,789,788 in coffee; so it would appear that coffee is the great staple, yielding in value nearly one half the island's exports.

This is an excellent thing for Puerto Rico, for the world's coffee-raising area is more restricted than that of sugar, or of almost any other agricultural product except tea. This means that the world's supply of coffee must always come from a region which is not susceptible of unlimited extension, as is the case with the cereals, etc. To the peculiar terrene and climatic conditions necessary to produce perfect tobacco, add another factor—that of altitude—essential to a perfect coffee, a combination that does not exist everywhere, even in the tropics.

The total value of the coffee imported into the United States in the fiscal year 1898 was, despite the low prices of the year, $65,067,561, against $60,507,630 in 1888, $51,914,605 in 1878, $25,-

288,451 in 1868, $18,369,840 in 1858, and $8,-249,997 in 1848. Thus the money sent abroad for coffee in the year just ended is eight times that of a half century ago, and nearly three times that of 1868. The cost of the coffee imported into the United States during the past ten years has been $875,494,241, these figures being the prices paid in the foreign markets at the port of exportation. Thus it appears that in the decade just ended there has gone out of the country an average of $87,500,-000 per annum for an article which may be successfully grown in all the islands now coming under the jurisdiction of the United States.

Practically one half of the coffee grown in the world now comes to the United States. The latest estimates put the coffee production of the world at 1,600,000,000 pounds per annum, while the imports into the United States last year were more than half that amount.

Of the total coffee production of the world, about two thirds is grown in Brazil, where an export duty of eleven per cent is placed on every pound of coffee exported. The other third of the world's production, which is grown outside of Brazil, is scattered around the globe in the belt extending to the thirtieth degree on each side of the equator, the most successful locations being well-watered mountain slopes from one to four thousand feet above sea level. The requisites for coffee production are found in all the islands now likely to come under control of the United States, while the fact that Brazil, the greatest coffee producer, places an export duty on all coffee exported, operates to the advantage of those desiring to enter upon the production of this article, either for home consumption or for competition in the markets of the world.

Puerto Rico has for years produced considerable coffee, this being her most important export, and amounting to from twenty-five to thirty million pounds per annum. Mr. F. B. Thurber, a well-known authority on this subject, says in his book, Coffee, from Plantation to Cup: " Puerto Rico furnishes a coffee that is in great favour in Spain and Italy and also on the island of Cuba. The cultivation is carried on largely in the provinces of Mayagüez, Ponce, Guayanilla, Aguadilla, Arecibo, and San Juan. In flavour this ranks as a mild coffee."

The coffee of Puerto Rico ranks with the best, and (though this may seem a reflection on our tastes) that is the reason it goes abroad and is not common in our marts. The finest coffee plantations are in the interior, and the south and west portions of the island, situated, as a rule, above an altitude of six hundred feet; but the newly introduced Liberian coffee will grow in the lowlands. As a cultivation, nothing can surpass this, taking one into the most beautiful parts of the island, where the heat of the lowlands is modified, where tree-ferns and bamboos wave their luxuriant fronds, where streams flow through tree-shaded valleys, and where the diseases of the littoral region rarely are endemic.

The coffee tree is a tender plant, requiring when young shade and protection from the winds, and these are secured by planting rows of bananas and plantains for the first and wind-breaks of large trees for the second. It will begin to bear in about three years, and continue to increase its yield for a dozen years thereafter. Planted at a distance of ten to twenty feet apart, the spaces between the trees may be utilized for "catch crops" of such vegetables as eddoes, yams, "pigeon peas," and sweet potatoes, while the sheltering banana plants themselves will yield a crop of fruit the second year, but should not be allowed to remain after the fourth.

The Arabian coffee does best at an average height above the sea of fifteen hundred to three thousand feet, and this is where, in those mountainous islands of the West Indies, climate, scenery, and hygienic conditions exist in perfection. The life of a coffee planter, however, is necessarily an isolated one, and it is a question whether many people can endure the environment of solitude, the absence of schools and society; but that depends upon individual tastes.

Planter's house, ceiba tree, and royal palms.

SUGAR, TOBACCO, COFFEE, AND CACAO. 65

A romantic story attaches to the introduction of coffee into the West Indies, all the subsequent groves, it is said, having been derived from a single plant, presented by a magistrate of Amsterdam to Louis XIV of France in 1714. The Dutch controlled the output of coffee then, and were very jealous lest it should spread to islands not in their possession, but plants from this parent tree were sent from France to Martinique. The voyage was long and the water gave out on board ship, but the botanist in charge deprived himself of half his allowance daily and shared it with the plants. From this small beginning grew the groves which now adorn not only the hill and mountain sides of Martinique, but of Puerto Rico.

As the coffee trees if allowed to grow will reach a height of from thirty or forty feet and as the best coffee grows at the top, it is necessary to cut them down to not more than six or eight feet, by which process they are made accessible to the pickers. They should also be vigorously pruned, or they will become masses of branches and less fruitful than if carefully trimmed.

The coffee fruit consists of two seeds inclosed in a sweetish pulp, the outside skin of which becomes red when ripe, when it should be picked or shaken from the tree. Of the two important varieties grown in the West Indies, the Liberian—found not many years ago in the forests of West Africa—is more hardy than the Arabian, which was originally derived from the mountains of Abyssinia. The crop will vary according to the number of trees per acre and the fertility of the soil, but from six to twelve hundred pounds per acre, or an average of a pound to a tree, is considered fair. The Liberian coffee, which, by the way, is less subject to the scale insect than the Arabian, is hardier and more prolific, sometimes yields to the amount of three to eight pounds per tree. Over in Haiti, it is said, the indolent negroes wait till the coffee falls from the tree, then scrape it up, with the dirt and leaves combined; but the best plan is to pick by hand as soon as ripe. A good picker can gather three bushels a day, which yields about thirty pounds of dry coffee. After picking, the fruit is taken to the "pulper," a machine in which the pulp is removed by being carried between a roller and a smooth surface. Then it is soaked in water to remove the mucilaginous matter adhering to it, then dried, and when thoroughly dry—not before—it may be passed beneath a heavy roller to remove the "parchment," after which it is winnowed and stored.

Coffee is an Old World product; from the New World comes the bean which yields that delicious

SUGAR, TOBACCO, COFFEE, AND CACAO.

beverage cacao, or chocolate. Its name indicates its indigenous origin, for from the Aztec *cacahuatl* was derived the name "chocolate," by which it is known to-day. Cacao is a native of tropical America, and was probably known to the aboriginal inhabitants of this island, as stones have been discovered which were evidently used for crushing the bean, or chocolate. The tree grows well in the coast country, but best in valleys from three to five hundred feet above the sea, where it can get abundant moisture and the washings of the hills. It reaches a height of twenty or thirty feet, but should be carefully pruned and thinned, so that it can be kept within bounds. When in bearing, the cacao pods grow from the limbs and branches, and also directly from the trunk itself, looking at a distance like great, swollen, red and purple rats climbing up the trees.

The seeds, from which the chocolate is obtained, are contained inside this pod, in a sweetish pulp, sometimes to the number of thirty or forty. They, are easily separable, and the cultivation of the cacao —taking one, as it does, to the fragrant valleys of the higher hills—would seem a very desirable occupation. At least one island, which was nearly ruined by clinging to the old-fashioned methods of sugar cultivation, was saved and eventually became wealthy by abandoning sugar and taking to cacao. This island is Grenada, in the southern West Indies; and there seems to be no reason why any other should not be equally benefited by following the same course.

The general cultivation, preparation of the land, etc., is similar to that employed in coffee culture, but the trees are not in full bearing under seven years, and do not yield much before five. So it will be well to utilize the waste land between rows with what are called " catch crops " of cassava, tannias, etc., bananas and plantains for the shade, and to set out quick-growing trees for wind-breaks. The average yield is from two to eight pounds per tree, and the various processes of fermenting, curing, " claying," etc., require experience—which may be gained from some native proprietor while the grove is growing.

VI.

FRUITS, SPICES, CEREALS, FOOD PLANTS.

OUR imports of fruits and nuts, it is estimated, "nearly all of them of tropical growth, and many of them from these very islands (Cuba and Puerto Rico)," amount to $17,000,000 every year; of fibres, jute, Sisal hemp, etc., to $12,000,000; and of cacao, to $3,000,000. As the fibre-plants can be produced in such relatively barren places as the Bahamas and Yucatan, where the soil is too poor for almost anything else, it is doubtful if it would be wise to attempt their cultivation in this island.

Respecting fruit culture and its future in Jamaica, a letter from that island, written in 1898, contains this item:

"The success of the Boston Fruit Company has been an object-lesson to the people of Jamaica that has not been unheeded. The Americans constituting this company have shown what can be accomplished by intelligent and thrifty enterprise, and have steadily extended the range of their cultivation, and have now so large an acreage established in fruit and purchase fruit to such a large extent that they are credited with maintaining in prosperity three of the fourteen parishes of the island.

"The question is agitating the people of those parishes whether under the changed conditions the Boston Fruit Company will not cease any further expansion in Jamaica, or will not even contract its operations and eventually abandon this island altogether and transfer all its enterprises and energy to Cuba. If the people should become convinced that the latter result is almost certain, unless Jamaica is placed on an equal status with Cuba with respect to the American market, the movement in favour of annexation would receive a mighty impetus."

Besides the fruits already mentioned there are the grape, date, fig, sapadilla, shaddock, citron, guava, mango, pomegranate, avocado pear, plum, tamarind, "cherry," star apple, mamie apple, acajou, or "cashew," granadilla, water lemon, bread-fruit, custard apple, sugar apple, sour sop, and others which grow wild, as the beach plum, the sea grape, etc.

A shrub which now practically runs wild is the guava, from which the delicious jelly is made. Old or neglected plantations soon become covered with guava bushes, which bear abundantly and might be made very profitable.

Owing to the absence of winter frosts and snows there is a perpetual succession of fruits and vegetables, and something may be planted, as well as harvested, every week and month in the year.

All these fruits are wholesome enough when eaten ripe and taken at the proper time of day, but much sickness is caused here by the eating of immature fruits, as well as from the same indiscretion in the temperate zone. Anent the frightful sickness prevalent in the ranks of our soldiers in Cuba, during their brief campaign in that island, a writer at the time says:

In the long list of suggestions from the medical department, all of which were disregarded, the ripe mango was recommended as a desirable article of diet. But somebody at headquarters issued an edict against it, and the soldiers were called up by the company commanders and told that if they ate the fruit they would be punished. This is the way the company commanders addressed their men:

"Now I see that some of you have been eating those mangos in spite of our advice to the contrary. Do you know what the Cubans call this fruit? They call it General Mango, because they say that the mango has killed more Spanish soldiers than all of their generals put together. If you eat it

General Mango will kill you, just as it has killed the Spaniards. I am told on good authority that if you eat a mango every day and then get yellow fever you will swell up frightfully and surely die. Now, I give you this positive order, that not one of you shall eat any of this fruit, and I shall punish severely any man that disobeys the order."

After such an order the obedient regulars generally let the mangos alone, although they were abundant, tempting, and delicious. The volunteers ate them more freely, without any bad result, so far as heard from. When the Cuban officers and aides were asked their opinion as to the wholesomeness of the fruit they generally said: "It is perfectly wholesome if eaten ripe; all these bad things apply to the unripe mango, which is sometimes eaten by the Spaniards." Most of the army doctors seemed to think that the only way to prevent the eating of the unripe mango was to prohibit the fruit altogether. There were many cases in which even the most obedient regulars were impelled by thirst and by the hunger for a bite of fruit to disobey the order; and as the clear yellow mango is always ripe, while the unripe fruit is green or greenish, it did not take a very high order of intelligence to discriminate between the fruit which was fit to eat and that which was unfit.

It is certainly hard to believe any ill of a mango when one looks at it. The tree itself is a most beautiful and attractive thing. Imagine a tree as large as a big oak, covered with rich and glossy foliage finer than that of the orange tree, and covered also with golden fruit nestling brilliantly among the green leaves. On such a tree there must often be a hundred bushels of mangos, fully matured, every one of which is as large as a good-sized pear. In shape the mango is not unlike a short and thick cucumber, and it has a thin, tough skin, which, when matured, reveals a mass of the most delicious juicy pulp. The only trouble about eating the mango is that one needs an ablution afterward. Some say that the ideal way is to get into a bath-tub, take the mango, eat it, and then go on with the bath. But one is perfectly willing to take the trouble to seek the ablution, for the sake of the fruit. And imagine the trees which bear the fruit growing wild everywhere, and also springing up in every garden and dooryard; the largest and finest ones were away up on a wild mountain side, where apparently no one had ever gathered the abounding fruit. Nor are they a native fruit in Cuba; they were introduced from India and have simply gone wild in the rich soil of the island.

A fruit which it will particularly pay to cultivate is the pineapple, discovered growing wild in the Bahamas by the first Spaniards to arrive here, and the native name of which has been adopted as its Latin generic appellation, *anana*. It is one of the many gifts of the New World to the Old, and is pronounced one of the most delicious fruits known to man. The West Indian coast-belt is its natural home, and here it flourishes as nowhere else, the pines of Jamaica, Antigua, and the Bahamas being celebrated for their luscious flavour. They will grow in almost any light, sandy, or gravelly soil, and even in the interstices of decomposed coral rock; in the Bahamas, indeed, it is said that holes for planting are made with a crowbar and seeds driven in with a shot-gun!

The pine, however, appreciates a rich, porous soil, and after the land is well cleared the plants may be set out in rows at from three to six feet apart; the latter distance is preferable, owing to the difficulty of cultivation, from the sharp spines of the plant. At six feet apart an acre will support twenty-five hundred plants, and at three feet five thousand. Although the pine will grow from seed as well as from the crown of leaves, detached, that tops the fruit, yet the best mode of propagation is by the suckers, which spring spontaneously from the parent plant. They thus reproduce themselves, like the banana and plantain, and on rich soil will grow for years and produce well, but fresh plants should be set out after three or four years. With proper attention to the selection of choice varieties, cultivation, and particularly packing for market, it is

A pineapple field.

believed that the culture of the pine will soon become a favourite one in the West Indies, because of its profits and the convenience to American markets.

Oranges, limes, lemons—all products of the citrus family, in fact—flourish here with little cultivation, and have not yet been considered of sufficient important to merit attention; but there is no doubt that they can be made very profitable. There are no frosts here, as occasionally in Florida; transportation to our Eastern seaboard, being by ship and steamer, would be less than railroad freights from California; so far as known, there is no obstacle to the free cultivation of all these fruits. The same may be said of pineapples—an uncertain crop in frosty countries—which grow almost spontaneously here, and to enormous size, with delicious flavour.

It was estimated by a writer on orange culture some years ago that the yield of that fruit in the United States gave an average of but one orange to each inhabitant, and when our population should have doubled it would require no less than thirty billion to furnish it with one orange per diem. And as the fruit of the citrus family only arrives at perfection in the tropics, there is every reason to believe that the West Indies will soon take the place of Mediterranean countries in furnishing our supply—because of their accessibility, of the comparatively short voyage necessary to market, and of the vast areas now covered with wild growths capable of being brought into cultivation.

These islands are the natural home of this family, and while the average yield of an orange tree may be estimated at from five hundred to one thousand in Florida and California, from three to eight thousand have frequently been taken from a single tree in the West Indies; in one island as high as fourteen thousand. Details of cultivation would be superfluous, in view of what has been published in recent years; and we will merely note that, allowing for difference in soils and climate, altitude, etc., the methods are the same, or ought to be, as prevail in Florida and California.

Lemons also, but particularly limes—those small golden balls of fruit filled with antiscorbutic juice —flourish in the West Indies at every altitude, preferring, however, sheltered valleys not far from the coast. While the lime is often shipped as a fruit, it has been found more economical to concentrate the juice and bottle or barrel it, and large fortunes have been made by the proprietors of lime estates in Jamaica, Dominica, Montserrat, and Trinidad,

FRUITS, SPICES, CEREALS, FOOD PLANTS. 77

where its cultivation has supplanted that of the sugar-cane.

There is one group of tropical products which, though cultivated in the East for centuries, has not received great attention as yet in the Occident. This comprises the spices—cinnamon, ginger, nutmeg, vanilla, clove, pepper—which have all been found to take kindly to the West Indian climate. In point of fact, there is one spice, pimento, which is native to these islands, Central and South America, and has been exported from Jamaica for many years to the amount of nearly half a million dollars annually.

As any one who has seen a "pimento-walk" will testify, there are few more beautiful objects in nature than a grove of pimento trees, such, for instance, as the groves of St. Ann's Parish, in Jamaica, the trees reaching a uniform height of thirty feet, their brown stems smooth and clean, their branches covered with glossy green leaves.

The pimento will grow on a poor soil and loves the slopes of seaboard hills and mountains, a hot climate, and dry atmosphere. It runs wild in many islands, and, in fact, the process of planting recommended by an authority is to " allow a piece of land in the neighbourhood of already existing pimento groves to become overgrown with bush, which in the course of time is found to contain numerous pimento seedlings, grown from seeds devoured by birds and deposited there. When the plants are of a certain size the bush is cleared and the pimento trees allowed to grow up. Small crops may be gathered within seven years from the seed, the increase being regular for many years." The berries, known as "allspice," are gathered green, the young branches to which they are attached being broken off by boys who climb the tree and thrown to girls and women, who pick off the berries and take them to the drying places. Ordinarily the berries on the "barbecues" are dried in the sun, but an improvement on this process is the use of the American fruit evaporator, especially during damp or rainy weather. This is the only care necessáry, and if prices for pimento were always good no crop could equal it, for the yield is often a hundred pounds to the tree.

The nutmeg probably surpasses the pimento as an article of commerce in constant demand, but requires more care in its growth and preparation for market. A native of the Eastern Spice Islands, when the Dutch first gained possessions there, and for a long time after, they absolutely controlled the market, and to insure uniformly high prices burned all the surplus, sometimes destroying millions of dollars' worth. But the French finally got hold of some plants and took them to Cayenne, and a certain species of pigeon carried the nutmegs themselves to other islands in their crops, so that the Dutch monopoly was broken.

The tree grows to a height of thirty to fifty feet and is diœcious, so that care must be taken to have the majority of trees in a grove females, and the males should be planted, as far as possible, to the windward of the former, to insure perfect pollination. The nutmeg likes a hot, moist climate and a rich virgin soil, in a sheltered situation, and may be propagated from seed, either sown in nurseries or planted in the field twenty-five to thirty feet apart. It will begin to bear in the sixth or seventh year, the nut becoming ripe six months after the flower appears. The ripe fruit is a beautiful object, resembling somewhat an apricot on the outside, which bursts in two and discloses the dark nut covered with the *aril* or mace, which is of a brilliant scarlet. This is stripped off and pressed flat; the shells are broken open when perfectly dry and the nuts powdered with lime to prevent the attacks of worms, and sometimes smoked to preserve them. Sometimes twenty thousand nuts are obtained from a tree, with about three pounds of mace to every thousand nuts. There are botanic gardens in St. Vincent, Jamaica, and Trinidad in which all kinds of tropical fruits and nuts have been experimented with, also in Martinique and Guadeloupe, but none, so far as known, in Cuba or Puerto Rico—that is, no experimental gardens for the benefit of the people, as in the English and French islands. It is to the persistent efforts of the English and French in this direction that the world owes so much of its economic botanical knowledge to-day.

Another native of the Spice Islands has been successfully grown here—in these islands—for more than a hundred years, and that is the clove. A gentleman resident in Dominica secured some plants from Cayenne in 1789, and one of the original trees is said to be living yet in that island. The general cultivation is like that of the nutmeg, but the clove, being the unexpanded flower, is beaten from the branches as soon as the buds have turned from green to red. The trees will grow to a height of thirty feet and begin to bear in the fifth or sixth year, an average of five to ten pounds of cloves per tree being expected. These are dried in the sun, sometimes smoked to give them color, and require very little care, except to be kept from dampness.

Another spicy product is cinnamon, which may be grown anywhere in the islands up to fifteen hundred feet above the sea, and is not particular about soil or situation. The best cinnamon is obtained from the shoots, and should yield to the amount of two hundred pounds of the prepared bark to the acre.

Jamaica ginger is known the wide world over, not because it is a peculiar product of that island, however, for the plant is a native of the far East. It grows equally well in all the islands so long as the climate is hot and moist and the soil rich. The " ginger " lies in the underground stems of the plant, or the *rhizomes*, and to propagate it the latter are divided into small pieces and planted in well-prepared soil in the month of March or April. The plant will flower in September, but the rhizomes should not be dug before the following January or February, when they are turned out of the soil after the manner of potatoes, yielding a crop, under favourable circumstances, of some four thousand pounds to the acre.

Pepper and vanilla are the products of two very different vines, the one native to the islands of the Malayan Archipelago, the other to the forests of Central America, but both find a soil and climate adapted to their needs in the damp lowlands of the West Indies. The climate must be hot and humid; for the vanilla shelter and shade are desirable, and both yield very profitable crops. But one requires a special training in tropical horticulture to bring them to perfection, as well as skill and experience to cure and pack them properly.

The same, in truth, may be said of all the plants that have been enumerated; but the design of these chapters is more to call attention to what may be produced, rather than how to produce it, the author not claiming to be an expert in tropical agriculture.

The native vegetables are the yam, eddoe, sweet potato, cassava, cucumber, pea, beans, carrot, egg-plant, tomato, corn (maize), ochra, yucca, pumpkins, arrow-root in the higher regions, potatoes, cabbages, etc. As a rule, northern vegetables do not thrive here, unless high up in the hills, and then should be raised from northern-grown seed.

Some kinds of melons, including the *sandia*, or watermelon, may be raised here, and a few northern vegetables, but potatoes will not do well at a lesser altitude than at least two thousand feet above the sea. As for berries and the small fruits of the temperate zone, they are conspicuous mainly by their absence. The writer, however, has picked wild strawberries in the Blue Mountains of Jamaica.

Indian corn, or maize, is indigenous here, having been found in use by all the aborigines, growing everywhere, in all kinds of rich soil and at all altitudes; but other cereals, as wheat, oats, and barley, will not grow here, all flour and breadstuffs being imported from the north.

There is a variety of millet, known as Guinea corn, which, though a native of India, does remarkably well in the islands. The same may be said of rice, both the swamp and mountain variety, though the latter is the kind most in cultivation, and yields enormously.

The food plants, so called, such as the yam, sweet potato, cassava, arrow-root, tanier, etc., yield abundantly and are the real friends of the agriculturist with limited means.

When the Indians were first seen by Europeans they had in their gardens a peculiar shrubby plant with knotty stems, the roots of which expanded into tubers, known as *cassava*. There are two kinds, the sweet and the bitter, the former being used freely as a vegetable for the table; the latter poisonous and necessitating special preparation to prepare it for the table, the poisonous principle being dissipated only by heat. As enormous crops of the bitter cassava can be raised, it is a favourite plant for cultivation, for from it is obtained a fine quality of flour or meal—*farine*—also starch tapioca, and *cassareep*, which last named is the basis of the well-known West Indian " pepper pot."

Arrow-root, now chiefly produced in the Bermudas and St. Vincent, both English islands, ought to flourish in Puerto Rico and Cuba as well; in fact, everywhere in a hill country with good soil and tropical or subtropical climate. As much depends upon the care used in the preparation of the starch, the returns per acre can not be estimated with accuracy, but in ordinary cases they are large.

Another vegetable peculiar to the tropics is the tanier, or eddoe—the " taro " of the South Sea islands—which has tuberous rhizomes of large size, from which excellent starch is made, and which are very fine for the table, being considered among the " most valuable food plants of the West Indies."

To recapitulate the chief products of Puerto Rico and their range of cultivation: Along the coast the cocoa palm, the banana, pineapple, all tropical fruits and vegetables. The sugar-cane, up to 2,500 feet, under favourable conditions matures in from eleven to fourteen months and reproduces itself during five to ten years thereafter.

The cotton plant flourishes here also within the same belt, produces in from seven to nine months, and endures for three or four years.

FRUITS, SPICES, CEREALS, FOOD PLANTS.

The manioc, or cassava, likewise lives in this belt and is a very profitable plant for the cultivator.

Maize—from the aboriginal Haitian name of which the Latin specific appellation is derived, *mayz* or *mahiz*—is found everywhere from the coast line to 3,000 feet above the sea, ripens its corn in from three to five months, and requires planting annually.

Tobacco, which grows within the same area, also requires annual planting and matures within six months from the seed.

Coffee and cacao grow anywhere above six hundred feet—the former best above one thousand to fifteen hundred feet—demand from three to five years for their first crops, and endure for forty years or more.

VII.

DYES, DRUGS, WOODS, AND MINERALS.

BOUNTEOUS Nature certainly intended the West Indian islands to be well provided with all tropical products of the vegetable kingdom, for there are more than it will be possible to enumerate. Our pharmacopœias, for instance, are deeply indebted to the American tropics for many of their "medicaments," such as guaiacum, aloes, sarsaparilla, jalap, castor bean, etc., all of which flourish here. Then there are trees and shrubs valuable for their gums, such as the copal, the "mamey," and the great gum trees of the "high woods," the exudations from which are used as incense in some of the churches.

Many plants, the bark, fruits, or wood of which are used in dyeing and tanning—as the indigo, turmeric anatto, and the "divi-divi," or *cæsalpinia*—grow here practically in a wild state.

To these may be added the cinchona and the coca, from the mountains of South America, and even tea from the hill countries of China. In the mountains of Jamaica large plantations of cinchona may be seen at an elevation of from four to six thousand feet, which have been set out under the auspices of the Government in the hope of introducing a new culture into the West Indies. It can not be said that it has been a great success, though the product of the cinchona, quinine, is in constant demand all over the world. The tree grows well in a rich forest soil, such as is found in all the mountainous islands, and anywhere above two thousand feet elevation. The first crop of bark is gathered after four years, when the trees are thinned out, but the main harvest occurs after the seventh year. As the root bark is richer in alkaloids than that of the trunk or branches, the trees are often grubbed up; but there are other methods, by which the tree is preserved, and at the same time the bark is gathered, such as by lopping off the branches and shaving off the outer bark in strips or ribbons.

Another South American product which has been introduced into the West Indies with some success is coca (*Erythroxylon coca*), from the dried leaves of which is obtained the drug which has come into use as a tonic, and the alkaloid known as *cocaine*, which has the property of rendering the tissues of the body insensible to pain. It is a hardy shrub and will grow almost anywhere, can be propagated from seedlings or cuttings, and will yield a harvest in eighteen months from the time of planting.

There is no good reason why tea culture should not succeed in Puerto Rico, for the plant has taken very kindly to the West Indian climate, a small plantation having been set out some years ago in Jamaica, from which tea of excellent quality has been obtained. Full directions for its culture are issued by the Government, and doubtless could be had upon application, as well as for the cinchona and coca and other rare plants, the cultivation of which is yet in the experimental stage in the West Indies.

Among the medicinal plants we must reckon the " palma christi," since from its seeds is obtained the well-known castor-oil; but though the oil has both an economic and medicinal value and the cultivation is the simplest, yet the plant itself is ranked as little more than a weed, growing wild in waste places and being perennial.

The jalap, a beautiful climbing plant, native of Mexico, thrives well in the West Indies, doing best in the rich humus of mountain forests at an elevation of from three to five thousand feet above the sea, where the mean temperature is about 60° to 70°. Crops of tubercules are gathered the third year after planting, and yield, when dried, about a thousand pounds to the acre.

A somewhat similar plant is the sarsaparilla, a native of Central America, but cultivable in the islands, which will grow anywhere in the lowlands and is easy of culture. The crop may be harvested, the roots dug up, after two years and annually thereafter. According to the government botanist of Jamaica, the first crops there yield as high as twenty pounds of dried roots per plant.

Of vegetable substances used in dyeing, none was better known in ancient times than indigo, by the cultivation of which many West Indian planters amassed immense fortunes; but, like the cochineal of Mexico, it has been mainly superseded by aniline colours, and its culture, no longer profitable, has been abandoned, the plant running wild in many regions.

A common but now neglected plant is the anatto—the *Bixa orellana*—which is in such repute with some farmers for colouring their butter, and which was used by the ancient Indians to colour their skins. The anatto shrub grows to the size of a quince tree, has heart-shaped leaves and rose-coloured flowers, followed by bristly pods, something like chestnut burs, and which burst open when ripe, displaying a crimson pulp containing numerous seeds. This pulp is immersed in water for a few weeks, strained, then boiled to a paste and formed into cakes, which are dried in the sun.

As the Caribs of the West Indies used the *roucou*, or anatto, to colour their skins, so the natives of the Polynesian islands are said to have used the turmeric (*Curcuma longa*) to heighten their complexion, only in the one instance the native painted himself red, and in the other yellow. The Orientals also use turmeric as a condiment, as an ingredient in the universally used curry powders, and as an aromatic tonic; but its use in the Americas is not yet prevalent.

As to logwood, which was introduced into the West Indies early in the last century, a learned writer on tropical agriculture advocates the planting of waste lands with it, as it will grow to commercial size in ten years. England imports it to the amount of nearly a million dollars annually, and in Jamaica it is so highly prized that the old roots are grubbed up that pertained to trees cut down many years ago. As an astringent in medicine and as a dye of commerce logwood is well known, being used also in compounding degraded clarets in France and her colonies. The tree is of low growth, rarely reaching forty feet in height, gnarled and twisted, and may be found near the coast as well as far in the interior. The heart-wood is deep red in colour and takes a high polish, and this portion is also that which contains the tincture, the light sapwood being chipped off as valueless, and the valuable portion sent to market in billets about three feet in length. Even the chips are valuable, and worth packing in bales for export.

We send abroad annually two million dollars each for indigo and cabinet woods, which this island can to a certain extent supply for years to come, or rather after a wise system of replanting and reafforesting has been carried out; basing future estimates upon what it has produced in the past.

For raw silk, our chief of the Government Bureau of Statistics says we send away twenty-five million dollars annually. In the sheltered valleys of Puerto Rico's mountains the mulberry finds a congenial home, the silkworm likewise, and neither winter snows nor high-priced labour will make silk culture difficult. It is not known that experiments have been conducted here, but in Cuba, where soil and climatic conditions are similar, the "mulberry grows to perfection, and the silkworms are more prolific and productive than in any other part of the world."

There are many natural productions, some already mentioned, which may well be classed as spontaneous growths; the forests particularly contain trees which have been sought for centuries as most precious dye and cabinet woods, chief of which are the logwood, mahogany, fragrant cedar—such as the Cuban cigar boxes are made from—the laurel, boxwood, and walnut. Add to these the oak, locust, gum tree, the palms (various species), the "tobacco wood," lignum-vitæ, the towering *ceiba*, or silk-cotton, which spreads over an enormous surface and is a magnificent tree, and numerous species unknown in the north.

In the island of Vieques are forests of these woods, and some remnants left on the mountains; and that some of them have been appreciated in times past, it is only necessary to repeat what dealers generally know, that the island mahogany of Cuba, Puerto Rico, and Santo Domingo is held in higher esteem than that from Honduras, logs having been shipped worth five thousand dollars each landed in London.

Most of the agricultural products are of the littoral lands, but the rare woods are found at higher levels. Ascend now toward the central ridge of mountains, or climb the bench of fertile land above Mayagüez on the west coast. All the way you are accompanied by the bamboos, whose feathery-foliaged lances, like great spears clashing in the wind, are now elements in the West Indian landscape which are purely tropical in character. The bamboos serve a variety of uses, and are especially valuable in hut-building and in fencing, being sometimes sixty feet in length, almost as strong as iron and smooth as glass. Even the palm hardly surpasses the bamboo in the variety of uses it is put to by the natives of the tropics, for besides serving to frame and thatch his hut, furnish mats, hats, fishing-poles, canes, poles for masts, even fibre for coarse sails, it also yields a tender terminal bud, like the palm, which when very young may be eaten like asparagus. But it is to the horticulturist that the bamboo is especially serviceable, for the long stems being hollow and the nodes or knots from ten to fourteen inches apart, with a thin partition at every node, these joints are made use of as flower pots, for which they are well adapted. The pots thus made at no expense are light, durable, and covered with a silicious glaze that makes them impervious to water. They are used in the nurseries of the coffee plantations, and thus save much expense that would otherwise be necessary if earthen pots were used, being split open with a blow of the cutlass when the plant is removed, or emptied of their contents and thrown away.

Another hill lover, which, like the bamboo, was originally introduced from foreign parts, is the bread-fruit (*Artocarpus incisa*), brought to the West Indies from the South Sea Islands little more than a century ago, but now abundant in the French and English islands. It is so abundant, in fact, as to have become the sugar-planters' bane, for the blacks will not work while the bread-fruit is ripe— and that is pretty much all the time—for its fruit is one of the most delightful and satisfactory foods that a hungry man could desire. Many is the time the writer has made a meal of half-wild bread-fruit gathered in the hills, roasted in the ashes of his camp-fire, and made palatable by sauce of hunger and salt of appetite. With its rugged trunk and deeply lobed leaves, the bread-fruit is an ornamental as well as useful tree, and fits well into its environment.

Reaching an altitude greater than two thousand feet above the sea, we find that all extensive agricultural operations cease, and in the place of large plantations the primitive " provision grounds," as they are called in the English islands, of the poor natives, where they grow small fruits and vegetables. But from this elevation on, we have with us and around

The bread-fruit.

us the glorious vegetation of the "high woods," where the beautiful tree-ferns wave their lacelike fronds, mountain palms thrust their domed heads through green masses of epiphytic plants, and gigantic gum trees tower aloft, wreathed and bound together by wonderful lianas, or water vines.

The natural resources of Puerto Rico are by no means confined to the vegetable kingdom, for anciently mines of gold were worked by natives under Spanish overseers; copper, iron, zinc, and coal have been found here; quarries of excellent gypsum are still open in the eastern part of the island, and the littoral lands abound in salt mines.

Now that the last of Spain's possessions in America has been wrested from her; now that all save the Spanish habitudes, language, and traditions are to be blotted from the western hemisphere, leaving her no material holdings, she may well believe that Columbus was her evil genius, rather than her beneficent saint and saviour. She has battled and toiled, poured out treasure and sweated away the very life blood of her people, for nearly four centuries past, yet what remains to her now?

Nothing, worse than nothing; for she has impoverished her land that her colonies might thrive —a land itself rich in material resources, capable of supporting a vastly greater population than it does, yet covered with deserted estates, filled with beggars, and perishing with the dry rot of corrupt bureaucracy.

When the first gold arrived in Spain, taken thither by Columbus—some of which may be seen to-day on the high altar of the Carthusian convent at Burgos—the rulers took it as an earnest of millions to come. Millions more did come, but were spent by Isabella and Ferdinand, Charles I, and lastly by Philip II. Toward the end of the sixteenth century it ceased to flow into the coffers of Spain—that golden stream—but while it lasted that country revelled and rioted in extravagance, indulged in costly wars that convulsed all Europe and scattered broadcast what had been gathered at the expense of thousands of human lives. Meanwhile, the resources of the home country had been neglected, the people had become demoralized, and Spain became dependent upon her colonies for everything. When these were taken from her, one by one, she sank lower and lower, until now, it would seem, she could touch no greater depth of degradation. Yet it was a sailor in the employ of Spain who carried the first American gold to Europe; a soldier of her army who discovered the largest nugget ever found in the New World; and officers of the royal command who plundered the palaces of Montezuma and the Incas.

The first glimpse of gold was obtained at San Salvador, in the Bahamas, and when the natives were asked whence it came they pointed to the south and west. So Columbus, when he later made the north coast of Cuba, was ever mindful of the gold region, and gave instructions to the captain of the expedition he sent into the interior to be sure to ascertain from the Grand Khan (whom he supposed to reside there) where it was located. But he discovered no gold in Cuba, other than a few pieces wrought into ornaments, and it was not until he and his caravels had arrived off the coast of Haiti, in the latter part of December, 1492, that he heard of a region rich in gold.

He had been all along, and still was, sailing toward what he supposed was the country mentioned by the learned Marco Polo as the kingdom of the Grand Khan, and known as Cipango. And when, in the bay of Acul, on the north coast of Haiti, the hospitable cacique Guacanagari, one of the Indians of that section, made Columbus a present of a cotton girdle, attached to which was a mask, with ears, nose, and tongue of beaten gold, he felt sure he had reached at last the country of Cipango; for, when questioned as to the location of the region whence they got the gold, the natives pointed westward and uttered the magical word *Cibao*. It may have sounded like Cipango; at all events, Columbus took it to be the same, and made all haste to reach it. He was, in fact, on his way to visit Chief Guacanagari, who lived on the shore of Cape Haytien's great bay, when his flagship, the Santa Maria, ran on a reef and became a total wreck. The Indians saved all the wreckage possible, and the cacique took the Spaniards to his village and entertained them with dances and feasting, in order to divert their minds as much as possible from their great calamity.

Thus the Spaniards passed their first American Christmas on shore; but in the afternoon Cacique Guacanagari made a visit of state to the little Niña, and while he was aboard, his simple subjects, dressed in the garb of nature, swarmed around the caravel in their dug-outs, holding up nuggets of gold, and crying out "Chug chug!" thus intimating that they wished to barter them for the hawk-bells which made the tinkling noise that ravished their unsophisticated ears.

Seeing that the gold gave the sailors great joy in its possession, Guacanagari assured Columbus that if that was all he wanted he would guide him to a region where the very stones were of the precious metal. At the same time he pointed west-

DYES, DRUGS, WOODS, AND MINERALS. 99

ward, and told his host that the heart of the golden country was *Cibao*—by which name it is called to-day, and the subsequent finding there of gold to the amount of millions proves that Guacanagari was no liar. At the banquet which he gave to Columbus on the following day he wore a golden coronet and nothing else, until the admiral presented him with a shirt and a pair of gloves. Guacanagari proved the truth of that old proverb about a crown being particularly burdensome when you want to rest, by " shucking " his coronet, after he had imbibed several draughts of fire-water, and his two sub-chiefs did the same; so that when Columbus wrote his sovereigns, several days later, that he fully expected the men he left there to collect a ton of gold during his absence, he had every reason to believe they would do so.

Taking final leave of the gallant Guacanagari, the Spaniards sailed westward, and on the evening of the 4th of January, 1493, three hundred and fifty-five years before the discovery of gold in California, while filling their water casks at the mouth of a river, they noticed particles of gold adhering to the hoops of their casks. The sands also glittered with gold, some of which they collected, and Columbus named the stream *Rio del Oro*, or River of Gold. It is known to-day as the Yaqui, and the place where Columbus anchored is not far from Monte Christi, on the north coast of Santo Domingo.

He did not stop then to explore the river valley, but continued on, finally arriving in Spain. He returned with a large fleet in November of the same year, found the garrison massacred he had left at Navidad, and the Indians dispersed. In December he laid the foundation of the town of Isabella, on the north coast of Santo Domingo, selecting the site not because it was favourable or its harbour good, but because it lay nearest to Cibao, or the gold region. As soon as possible an expedition was sent over the mountains to the valley of the Yaqui, and the gold it brought back was sent to Spain by the returning fleet in 1494.

They called the Yaqui the River of Gold, from the circumstance of finding gold there the year before, and soon they proved it to be well named, for in the streams constituting its head waters they found, besides jasper and porphyry, flakes and grains of gold.

The Spaniards found a great deal of gold in the river sands, as well as in pockets, but nearly all were mere surface indications, and they never even touched the real sources of the treasure. As in the Yukon and Klondike districts to-day, what was found was only the washings from the great gold sources in the heart of the hills and mountains. Humboldt himself declared that though the Spaniards obtained what seemed to them a vast treasure of gold, from the West Indies and Mexico, South America and the Spanish Main, and their great galleons went home laden with nuggets and dust from many places, yet the fountain-head was never tapped. He likened these surface accumulations to the scattered flakes of a snowstorm, and what remained to the vast snow fields banked against the mountain sides.

The *Cibao* is in the region of pines, which indicates a high elevation, in an island so far south as Santo Domingo, and the air is sweet and pure. It is an ideal location for settlement or for mining, except that it is far away from all routes of travel, the nearest town to it being that of Santiago, on the banks of the Yaqui. The people here live most wretchedly, even though surrounded by a tropical exuberance of vegetation. They mainly depend upon the gold which they wash out of the streams for their daily needs, and they seem to have difficulty in summoning strength enough even for that. And yet the writer saw one native of Santo Tomas with a handful of nuggets, the largest of which weighed five ounces, all obtained from the river sands by washing with a wooden dish.

Such is the country in which the first gold was found in America four hundred years ago. The incidents attendant upon the finding of gold for the first time in Puerto Rico were similar to those in Santo Domingo; and, further, the same conditions prevail in both islands. The precious metal is found in the sands of rivers. It was very abundant in Ponce de Leon's time and still is found, but in lesser quantity. The mineral resources of Puerto Rico have not been fully exploited, if we may judge by the merely superficial investigations that have been made in the past four hundred years, for when De Leon arrived here, about 1509, many of the rivers poured down sands of gold; yet nobody has ascertained their source.

The Historia de Puerto Rico says: " Signs of gold have been found in many districts of the island, and auriferous sands in such rivers as the Luquillo, Sebuco, Daguao, Mayagüez, Manaron, and many others. Traces of gold in the neighbourhood of San Germán, Yauco " (at the port of which, Guanico, our troops first landed in Puerto Rico), " and throughout all the territory of Coamo, in such quantities as presupposes a vast abundance in reserve, but mostly in the south and west." Now, this report was made in the year 1788, or more than a hundred years ago, yet it holds good in substance to-day.

Though there may not be any large area of Crown land thrown open to new-comers, and though much, if not most, of Puerto Rico's lands are taken up, yet there will be a chance for the prospector, and possibly great discoveries may be made. His only expense, if he pursue the primitive operations of the natives, will be a wooden pan, costing a few cents, and the food necessary for his subsistence while wading the tropical streams.

At all events, if little gold rewards the adventurer in Puerto Rico's mountains, he will not be subjected to the rigours of an arctic climate, nor have to endure the severities of a trip to the Klondike. He will be able to work all the year through, if so inclined; the worst of his foes being mostly avoidable, such as malarial fevers, poisonous insects, and torrential rains.

VIII.

NATURAL HISTORY, GAME, INSECT PESTS.

THE island of Puerto Rico can hardly be termed a paradise for sportsmen, for the largest native quadruped there is the agouti, a small animal of the size and habits of a hare, a vegetarian, and good "eating" withal. He inhabits the rocky hillsides and borders of the woods, has a glossy brown coat of hair, and a sharp, sensitive nose, which he is constantly sticking up into the air and sniffing for danger; for he is a shy, timid little creature, whose life no one but a brute would take, unless hard pushed for food.

Then there is the armadillo, with a shell on his back, into which he promptly retreats at the first sign of danger. His "meat" is as tender as his horny covering is hard and impenetrable, and very delicious indeed when properly cooked and served in that same shell with the concomitant sauces and condiments. Sir Walter Raleigh, one of the first to mention this quaint animal, made its acquaintance at Trinidad, where, he says, "one of the Indians gave me a beaste called by the Spaniards *Armadilla*, and which they call *Cassacam*, which seemeth to be all barred over with small plates, somewhat like unto a *Rinocero*" (rhinoceros), " with a white horne growing in his hinder partes, as big as a great hunting horne, which they use to winde " (blow) " instead of a trumpet. Monardus writeth that a little of the powder of that horne, put into the eare, cureth deafness."

In the English islands he is called by the negroes *hag-in-ahmah* (a hog in armour), and in the French *tatouy*, his generic Latin name being *Tatusia;* but by whatever name he is known he is most excellent for the table when " shucked " out of his shell and served aright. It is not an easy matter to catch him, though, as he can dig a hole in the ground almost as fast as a stout labourer can excavate with spade and pick, and sometimes " doubles " underground like a fox pursued by the hounds.

Then there is the iguana, like a small-sized alligator, which, however, prefers to inhabit trees and bushes to dwelling in the water. It is savage in appearance but timid by nature, and will not fight unless cornered, when it will lash out terrifically with its tail and close its jaws like a vice upon whatever gets in the way. Though hideous of aspect, there are many worse things for the camp cuisine than stewed iguana when one is dwelling in the woods, as the writer can testify, for the flesh looks like the meat of quail and tastes like chicken.

In the forests and hills may be found the land crabs, than which there is nothing more delicious, except it be the *camarones*, or crayfish, fresh from the mountain streams, served on clean plantain leaves and with a dash of pepper and lime-juice. The crabs perform an annual migration between the mountains and the shore, and then may be captured by hundreds. But one should be careful and not mistake for them the bloated crustaceans dwelling along shore and near settlements, as these latter are carrion feeders, subsisting on garbage and graveyards. Salt-water shellfish are abundant, the muscles good, and the oysters eatable, but, like all warm-water products of their class, insipid and "coppery."

As for fish, some of the large streams yield good fresh-water varieties, and the coasts swarm with "shad," bonitos, bream, sardines, Spanish mackerel, snappers, dolphins, flying fish, sting rays, and sharks.

As a naturalist has asserted that the surrounding waters of Cuba possess some six hundred distinct species, it is probable that there are as many

Edible crabs on sale.

in the waters bathing Puerto Rico's shores. To these we may add such denizens of the deep generally classed with fish as the manatee and whales. The former was at one time abundant on the coast of Florida, and in the time of Columbus was known as the veritable mermaid. The great navigator, in fact, gravely asserts, in his journal, that he saw several manatees off the coast of Haiti, but was disappointed that those mermaids were not as beautiful as they had been represented to be!

The best fishing grounds are said to be in the magnificent bay of Aguadilla, on the west coast, and the harbour of Arroyo, on the south. All these waters swarm with fish of gaudiest colours, rainbow-hued, and of strangest shapes; but notwithstanding their abundance, the people of all the West Indian islands import great quantities of northern cod, dried and salted. With a shred of salt cod and a bit of bread-fruit, washed down with a drink of rum or cocoa water, the average Caribbean negro has "no use" for work, for his wants are satisfied.

Of real game birds there are very few, except for such stray Guinea fowl as may have run wild, migrant pigeons, *cordoniz*, or quail—which are really ground doves—parrots, seafowl, plover during the autumn migrations, snipe, duck, coots, gallinules, doves, etc. But a Guinea bird run wild is no mean substitute for the genuine article, as it affords the finest sport in the world, being as swift of foot and as wary and alert as a fox, and as strong of wing as a grouse. Some of the best " sport " in the West Indies may be had on the little-known island of Barbuda, north of Antigua, where are wild Guinea fowl in enormous flocks, wild fallow deer, goats, and sheep, besides doves and pigeons without number. But the West Indies do not afford, in general, large game for the mighty hunter. There are some deer in Cuba, perhaps a few in Puerto Rico, also wild boars, wild turkeys (not native, but domestic fowl which have taken to the woods); in the islands of Tobago and Trinidad are herds of savage peccaries, which are the only dangerous four-footed animals in the archipelago.

The best shooting is in the season when the spice trees ripen their fruit and the sea grapes and plums are plentiful. Then the hunter may take his stand beneath certain trees in the high woods or ramble through the thickets of sea grapes with a certainty of getting all he can carry of the fine white-headed pigeons, as large as a passenger pigeon and much plumper. The best time to hunt is in the winter season, usually, and the time of day very early in the morning or late in the afternoon.

Even the song and plumage birds are not very

plentiful, owing probably to the comparatively large areas of cleared lands and the recklessness of native gunners in destroying these innocent inhabitants of the woods and gardens. There are mocking-birds, with sweet song and vivacious air, troupials, wild canaries, sugar birds, several varieties of thrushes, owls, hawks, etc.—altogether perhaps one hundred and fifty species of birds are found in the island. Few in species, but many in number, are those gems of the air, the humming birds, which will enliven your flower garden—if you have one—all the year. And incidentally, without descending to particulars, it may be said that flowers bloom here in every month of the year, their variety only limited by the number of species in the tropical flora, which is vast and varied.

There are no wild animals, then, large enough to cause alarm; there are no poisonous serpents, and the boa found in the island does not exceed a dozen feet in length, and is looked upon with more of favour than aversion, because of its rat-killing propensities. Anent the snakes of the West Indies, the old historian, Bryan Edwards, says quaintly: "If it be true, as it hath been asserted, that in most of the region of the torrid zone the heat of the sun is, as it were, reflected in the untamable fierceness of their wild beasts and in the exalted rage and venom of the numerous serpents with which they are infested, the Sovereign Disposer of all things hath regarded the islands of the West Indies with peculiar favour, inasmuch as their serpents are wholly destitute of poison, and they possess no animal of prey to desolate their vallies." Another famous historian is said to have disposed of a similar subject, when writing the history of another country, by merely remarking, "There are no snakes in Ireland!"

Still, there are poisonous snakes in the West Indies, though there may be none in Puerto Rico. Even at the time Mr. Edwards was writing his excellent history of the islands, which was exactly one hundred years ago, there existed, in at least two islands of the archipelago, the most poisonous serpent known to the western hemisphere—the terrible *fer-de-lance*, so abundant and so deadly in the islands of Martinique and St. Lucia. It may have been brought from the Spanish Main, either by the invading Caribs, centuries ago, or may have drifted hither on floating vegetation torn from the tropical forests and borne northward by the Orinoco current—but there it is. A peculiar problem in the study of animal distribution which has apparently been neglected by naturalists is, how these two islands became infested with this venomous ser-

NATURAL HISTORY, GAME, INSECT PESTS. 111

pent, while other isles immediately adjacent, as Dominica to the north and St. Vincent to the south, are entirely free from them. The writer has hunted over all the islands of the Caribbees, but has never found a *fer-de-lance* outside the limits of Martinique and St. Lucia. It is even related that when the Caribs were at war with the whites, about a hundred years ago, they sought to introduce this serpent into Dominica, but without perceptible results, though the channel separating it from Martinique is but thirty miles in width.

In Trinidad and Tobago there are poisonous snakes, notably in the former; but these islands belong to the continental system of South America, as shown by their flora as well as their fauna.

As we have noticed some of the potential blessings which go to make of Puerto Rico an earthly paradise, it would be unfair to ignore the dangers which may be attendant upon the life of a dweller therein. One of the greatest evils of a tropical climate—consequent upon that continuous heat and moisture which bring forth and sustain an exuberant vegetation—is the abundance of insect pests. It is believed that Puerto Rico is as exempt as any country within the tropics, but that is speaking only relatively. The writer has passed many months in the tropical forests, hunting by day and sleeping by night beneath the palms and tree ferns, either without shelter or in a hastily-constructed *ajoupa*, or forest hut of plantain leaves; he has lived in the West Indies, summer and winter, several years, yet can say that he was never stung or bitten by anything more dangerous than an ant or a hornet. And this also was the experience of a veteran naturalist, the late Dr. Gundlach, of Havana, who spent sixty years in exploring the forests of Cuba, Puerto Rico, and other islands in the Caribbean. But that we came very near to danger many, many times, neither of us could deny, and it was more by good luck than anything else, perhaps, that we escaped.

Most to be avoided and dreaded are scorpions, tarantulas, centipeds, wasps, mosquitoes, black and red ants, wood-ticks, fleas, and chigoes. This last, generally called " a jigger," is also a flea, but not the " hop-skip-and-jump " variety, being known in Latin as the *Pulex penetrans*, sustaining about the same relation to the first as the Digger Indian to the Sioux or Apache. It penetrates the skin—preferably of the toes—and there lays a mass of eggs and snugly ensconces itself, or herself; and if eggs and jigger are not promptly ejected, trouble soon results, neglected cases having resulted in the loss of the toe, or even foot and leg. So long, however, as one bears in mind not to walk barefoot over damp floors or rotting wood, and if a tickling sensation is felt in the toe, to investigate at once, this insect may not be regarded as a terror.

The habits of the others are too well known to need repetition here, but it should be particularly remembered that the tropical scorpions are extremely venomous, the tarantulas aggressive, and the centipeds remarkably rapid in their movements. The writer can recall many encounters with these insect foes, as, for instance, once, in the botanical garden of Martinique, he poked a tarantula with a cane—a long cane, fortunately—and the ferocious spider sprang at his hand, barely missing it. At another time, when camped in the woods, he brushed a scorpion from his blanket; in Haiti one morning, on picking up an article of dress, a big centiped ran between his fingers; again, in Dominica, seeing a very large centiped, all of six inches in length, running up the wall of a hut, he tried to "mash" it with a slipper, when the thing actually disappeared, apparently without any visible means of escape.

Still, the little white, black, and yellow children run about naked until—well, until they can "look over a barrel," as the saying is in the West Indies, and they never seem afraid of insect foes;

at all events, are as healthy and happy as children anywhere else in the world.

One of their bugaboos, however, says a Spanish author, is the fierce, wild dog locally known as the *perro montes*, or *cimarron*, which is said to abound in the woods, whence it emerges in bands of half a dozen or more and preys upon sheep, pigs, and calves. It has never been known to attack man, but might, when pressed by hunger, prove dangerous to children.

While on the subject of things to be avoided it may be well to take cognizance of the prevalent diseases of the island. There are fevers, to be sure, but more a resultant of local causes than from the hot and humid atmosphere. Few of the coast towns are afflicted with yellow fever, which is almost unknown in the interior, and endemic in San Juan, the capital, only because the most ordinary rules of sanitation have been notoriously neglected. An officer of the United States army, returned from Puerto Rico, declared in an interview that, " while the island is a paradise at certain seasons of the year, the climate is almost entirely devoid of recuperating properties during the months in which the tropical fevers prevail, which are embraced in the rainy season. But worse than this is the total disregard

Ancient and modern sentry boxes, San Juan.

of the natives for health-giving sanitary conditions. In the close back yards of the residences and even of the best hotels of Ponce, the second city in size, may be seen piles of rubbish and filth lying within a few feet of the cisterns from which the water supply is obtained."

Cholera, dysentery, diarrhœa, are possible, probable—the first-named disease carrying off thirty thousand people in 1855—and are mostly consequent upon eating unripe fruit, drinking bad water, or the violation of ordinary hygienic rules. But as for boiling all water before drinking (as was advised by the sanitarians of our army in Cuba), keeping out of the sun, and never walking or riding at mid-day, etc.—these precautions are not necessary; at least the residents do not think they are, and many of them live to a green old age. But it is unsafe to expose yourself to rains, without opportunity for quickly changing, at least, the under garments, to wet the feet without soon after putting on dry stockings, or to eat or drink to excess.

IX.

SAN JUAN, THE CAPITAL.

IN the forefront of the island's history stand the names of Columbus, who discovered it in 1493, and of Ponce de Leon, who founded the first city about seventeen years later. The latter was governor of the eastern province of Santo Domingo during the viceroyalty of Don Diego Columbus, and when reports were brought him of the great fertility and mineral wealth of Borinquen—as the aborigines called the island—Ponce went over to investigate. He landed on the west coast, and there met the cacique, or chieftain, Agueynaba, who showed him such rich valleys and so many streams rippling over the golden sands, that the Spaniard lost no time in bringing over a strong force of soldiers and establishing himself in this new and promising country.

The town he founded was called Caparra, now known as Pueblo Viejo, not far distant, across the bay, from the capital city, San Juan, for the site of which it was soon after abandoned. San Juan,

SAN JUAN, THE CAPITAL. 117

the city which owes its origin to the enterprise of Ponce de Leon, occupies the western end of a small island on the north coast, about two miles and a half in length and half a mile in breadth. It is connected with the mainland by two bridges and a causeway defended by small forts; and, lying between its fine harbour and a chain of lagoons on one side, with the Atlantic on the other, its position, from a military point of view, is almost impregnable.

The natural advantages for defence were early seized upon, and the northwest end of the islet, which is bluff, even precipitous, is crowned by the famed Morro Castle, the initial fortification, which was completed in the year 1584. In general shape this old "castle" is an obtuse angle, with three tiers of batteries facing the sea, placed one above the other so that their fires will cross. The Morro is the citadel and is a small military town in itself, with barracks, chapel, bakehouse, immense water tanks, warehouses, officers' quarters, bombproofs, and dungeons by the sea. As in Havana, the *faro*, or light-tower, stands here, crowned with a first-class lantern and rising to a height of one hundred and seventy feet above sea level.

This ancient citadel is the beginning of the

wall which surrounds the city, completely inclosing it within a line of connected bastions, with moats, guarded gates, battlements, *fortalezas*, semi-bastions, projecting sentry turrets—in fact, all the defences of a walled town or city of the middle ages. On the Atlantic shore, which is steep and against which the heavy surges roll continuously, a wall of modern construction connects the Morro with the castle of San Cristobal, which faces oceanward and also guards the approaches from the mainland. This castle is entered by a ramp on the highest part of the hill, to the inequalities of which the fortification is accommodated. It can concentrate its fire in any direction, as it controls the city and inner harbour by the Caballero Fort with its twenty-two large guns. Stretching from harbour to sea front, San Cristobal dominates the inland approaches and has practically three tiers of batteries behind fortifications in great part cut out of the solid rock.

Though the fortifications as we find them now were planned in 1630 and nearly completed by 1641, yet San Cristobal in its entirety was not finished until just before the outbreak of the American Revolution, or about 1771. Still, with its outworks, consisting of a redan resting on the highest part of the glacis and called Fort Abanico, on account of its fan shape, its moats, and modern batteries, San Cristobal would have been a hard fort to storm and take had our soldiers been compelled to attack it.

Beginning at the southern projection of San Cristobal and following the sinuosities of the bay shore-line, we find a front of bastions, commencing with those of San Pedro and Santiago, the curtain being pierced by the España gate; then comes the bulwark of San Justo and the gate which forms an arch under the curtain, succeeded by the semi-bastion of the same name, the bastion of La Palma, the platform of Conception, to the semi-bastion and *fortaleza* of Santa Catalina, built about 1640, which supports the residence of the captain-general. Between the *fortaleza* and the semi-bastion of San Augustine, running northwest, we note the gate of San Juan, and then follows the platform of Santa Elena. The San Juan gate gives access to the glacis of San Felipe del Morro, between the captain-general's palace and the citadel.

These details will give one an idea of the completeness of this line of circumvallation; but in addition to the great stone walls, some of them nearly a hundred feet high, which inclose the city, there are the outlying forts of San Antonio and San Geronimo, which defend the bridges inland;

and on an islet off the harbour mouth is the small but strong fort of Canuelo, between which and the Morro, less than a thousand yards distant, all large ships must pass to make this port. A chain was formerly stretched between the Morro and Canuelos in war time, but during the recent war, and after the bombardment of San Juan by our fleet (which occurred May 12, 1898), a vessel was sunk there and the harbour mined. This wreck was found to effectually block the harbour by the United States cruiser New Orleans, which arrived at San Juan about the middle of August, 1898, soon after the protocol of peace was signed.

The intramural city is one of the oldest and quaintest in the New World, having been founded within a decade of the city of Santo Domingo, antedating Havana by six or seven years, St. Augustine by more than fifty years, and being contemporary with Baracoa and Santiago de Cuba. It is regularly laid out in squares, with six streets running parallel with its longer axis, and seven others crossing them at right angles, while two plazas and several smaller squares, called *plazuelas*, offer places for promenade and recreation.

Probably the largest structure within the walls is the Ballaja barracks, overlooking the parade grounds and covering, with its *patio*, a space of

77,700 square metres. The palace of the captain-general is an imposing edifice, and the "Casa Blanca," or ancient castle of the founder, Ponce de Leon, the oldest as well as most attractive, with its walled garden and surrounding palms, in the capital. Other important buildings are the city hall, the archiepiscopal palace, the theatre, the Jesuit college, military hospital, the church of Santo Domingo, the cathedral, with its spacious naves and altar of fine marbles, and the church of La Providencia, where may be seen *Nuestra Señora de los Remedios*, the special patroness of the island, with her fifteen-hundred-dollar cloak and her twenty-thousand-dollar collection of jewels.

There are private clubs and casinos, a spacious market place, and last, but by no means least, a cemetery, just under the northern wall, with a sentry turret jutting over the gate, which gives entrance through the glacis of the Morro. In this cemetery may be observed the peculiar methods of inhumation, by which the wealthy are placed in the stone cells of a vast "columbarium," against the wall of the fort, and the poorer classes merely buried in rented graves, from which they are ejected at the expiry of a short term of years.

The effluvia from this (practically intramural) cemetery, together with the emanations from the sinks and sewage, the filthy streets, and crowded dwellings, have hitherto made of San Juan what nature never intended it should be, with its elevated situation and its soil impervious to water, pure or foul—a possible plague centre for the breeding of tropical diseases. It is the only city in the island where yellow fever is said to have been endemic; but with the constantly blowing trade winds, which sweep across it from the ocean, and the swift sea current flowing through the harbour, there is no excuse whatever for these local conditions so favourable to contagious diseases.

The urban population is estimated at about twenty thousand, probably one half being negroes and people of mixed bloods. These are domiciled in about one thousand houses, not more than one half of which are over two stories in height, plainly but massively constructed of *mamposteria*, or stone and mortar, with flat roofs, jutting balconies, some with *miradores*, or open cupolas, and generally surrounding a *patio*, or inner court, where often a fountain and plat of flowers makes an attractive spot for the gathering of the family during hours of recreation. The architecture, in fact, is essentially Spanish, or Hispano-Moriscan, like that of Andalusia. The streets are narrow, the sidewalks, when they exist, relatively narrower, scarcely wide

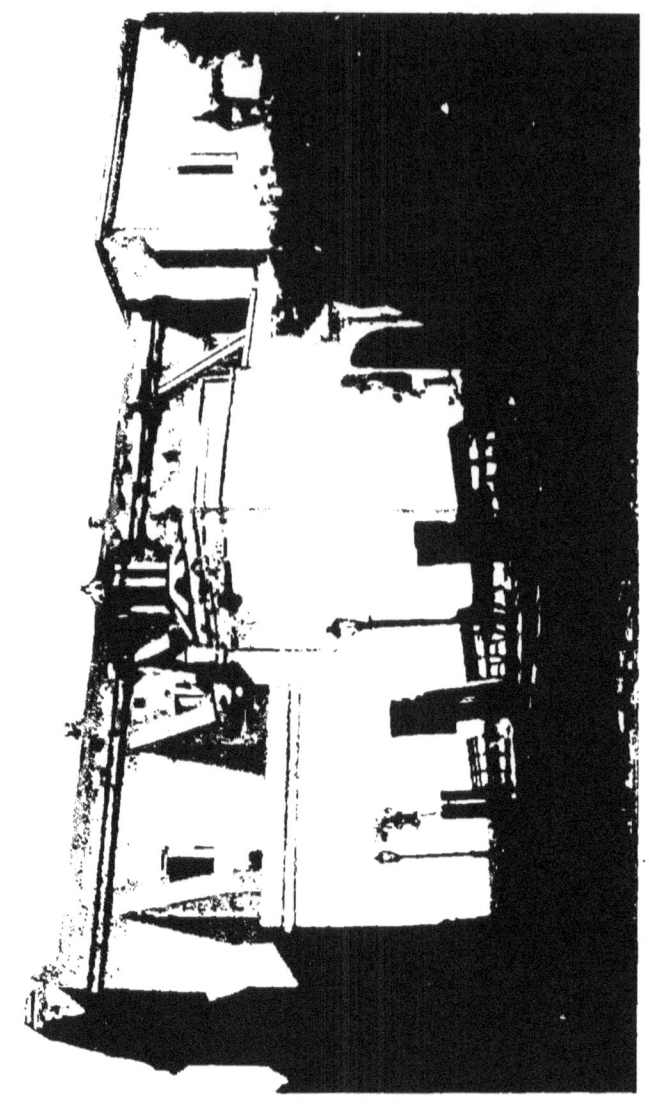

Church of Santo Domingo, San Juan.

enough for two persons to walk abreast, resembling much those of Obispo Street in Havana and some of the alleyways of Seville.

The supply of water is scanty, being derived mainly from the clouds and stored in cisterns, which, by the way, are for the most part in a state of neglect and very foul. When the city shall have become an American winter resort it is to be hoped that its system of sewage and sanitation will include the introduction of water from the hills not far away, where the supply is unlimited and of the purest quality.

Outside the walls are several suburbs, the two principal being known as the Marina and Puerta de Tierra, with perhaps seven thousand inhabitants between them, the total population pertaining to San Juan rising twenty-seven thousand. The Marina lies right up against the walls, with an overflow of garden and park filled with choice trees, shrubs, and flowers, dotted with kiosks and drinking booths, and with a broad avenue running out toward the mainland. Here are the wharves, also the custom house and many warehouses, while the most important building—not from its imposing architecture, but owing to the "functions" occurring there at stated intervals—is the cockpit, a ramshackle structure of stone and corrugated iron.

It is an easy descent from the city proper to the Marina, and every afternoon the walks and booths are occupied by pleasure-seeking people.

On the only road leading out to the mainland is the rambling hamlet of San Turce, and across the bay, reached by a local ferry, is Cataño, a village of little importance, but which affords a fine view of the capital.

Within the walls there are two small hotels, which, from the writer's experience, are rather to be shunned than sought, while boarding houses are altogether unknown. The first requisite for the American traveller, a good hotel, is yet to be built, while the stores and shops, though some of them contain good stocks of European goods, are wholly inadequate to the needs of a modern city. There are several good newspapers, published in Spanish, daily and weekly, but few manufactures here, nearly everything being imported. There are artificial-ice, gas, and electric-light works, and across the bay an establishment for the refining of crude petroleum, which is brought from the United States.

During perhaps eight months of the year San Juan affords an agreeable place of residence, the climate being mild and endurable; yet, owing to the changes from heat to cold at times, the prevalent diseases among the natives, it is said, are consumption, bronchitis, and catarrh. These, however, may be owing more to thoughtless exposure than to the inherent evils of the climate.

San Juan has honoured its founder, Juan Ponce de Leon, with a statue which stands in the centre of the Plaza Santiago. It was cast from cannon captured from the English in 1797, and is of the natural size, representing the great conquistador on foot, encouraging his soldiers to a charge. His remains are preserved in a leaden box, in the church of Santo Domingo, and the following is his epitaph:

Aqueste lugar estrecho
es sepulcro del varón
que en el nombre fué León
y mucho mas en el hecho.

The most ancient inscription reads:

AQUÍ YACE EL MUY ILUSTRE
SEÑOR JUAN PONCE DE LEÓN,
primer Adelantado de la Florida, primer Conquistador y Gobernador de esta Isla de San Juan.

X.
CITIES AND TOWNS OF THE COAST.

SAN JUAN is a port-of-call for the Spanish steamers between Cadiz and Cuba, and also for the intercolonial boats among the islands formerly pertaining to Spain, while an American line makes direct connection between this port and New York, touching as well at all important harbours on the coasts.

There is a life-saving and signal station at the Morro, and two submarine cables connect the island with the outside world—one via St. Thomas and the other through Kingston, Jamaica.

The insular system of telegraph lines aggregates five hundred miles and connects all important points, while a telephone service is in process of "installation," or will be in operation by the time these data are in print.

A railroad was long since projected to connect all centres of population, the following portions having been completed: From San Juan, along the coast through Rio Piedras; Bayamon, Dorado, Are-

CITIES AND TOWNS OF THE COAST. 127

cibo, and Hatillo, to Camuy; Aguadilla, through Aguado, Rincón, Añasco, and Mayagüez, to Hormigueros. A branch of this railroad from Añasco, through San Sebastian, to Lares. Ponce, through Guayanilla, to Yauco. This latter railroad follows the southern coast line and is paralleled by a wagon road throughout its course. In one place the railroad and road run within a few hundred yards of the coast. According to the Statesman's Yearbook for 1898 there are in operation 137 miles of railroad, besides over 170 miles under construction.

1. San Juan to Rio Piedras, 11 kilometres, and to Carolina, 12 kilometres. Purchased by American capitalists and to be run by electricity.

2. San Juan to Bayamon, 14 kilometres; to Toa Baja, 15; to Dorado, 4; Vega Baja, 18; Manati, 12; Barceloneta, 17; to Arecíbo, 8; to Hatillo, 10; to Camuey, 2. Total, 100 kilometres.

3. Line from Aguadillo to Hormiguero, 58 kilometres, as follows: Aguadillo to Aguada, 6; Rincón, 8; Añasco, 16; Mayagüez, 15; to Hormiguero, 13 kilometres.

Line from Yauco to Ponce, 35 kilometres: Yauco to Guayanillo, 12; to Tallaboa, 8; to Ponce, 15.

137,422 passengers travelled on these lines during 1896, about 16.5 per cent more than in 1895.

The gross receipts increased by $18,262 over those in 1895, and amounted to $251,191.

The scenery around San Juan, as well as of the entire island, is picturesque in the extreme, and even the casual visitor should not fail to visit the suburban hamlet of Cangrejos, where the wealthy merchants and foreign consuls reside; Rio Piedras, a pretty village a little way inland; Cataño, across the bay; and Bayamon, farther up the hills. If possible, take the *diligencia* over the magnificent highway between San Juan and Ponce, seventy miles or so, which climbs the slopes, winds through gorges and over mountains, across vast sugar estates, and past purling streams, with bits of tropical scenery that are worth going far to see, and glimpses of life and people peculiar to this mountainous island in the tropic seas.

The principal centres of population are along the coast, and to show that this island is by no means destitute of towns and cities, the chief of them will be enumerated. Due west from San Juan, on a river of the same name, lies Arecibo, about thirty-five miles in a direct line from the capital, and fifty by rail. It contains about six thousand inhabitants, and the district within its jurisdiction some thirty thousand; a well-built town, with a fine church and public buildings, a plaza, with streets running from it forming regular squares, a theatre, jail, and spacious barracks for the troops.

A tienda, or small shop.

CITIES AND TOWNS OF THE COAST. 129

Connected by rail with San Juan, and with telegraph and post office it may, in spite of its poor harbour, become an important city in the near future, for it lies at the entrance of a river, shallow but picturesque, and at the mouth of a valley famed for its natural beauties.

The environs are extremely picturesque, and have a peculiar feature which renders them worthy of a visit. About seven miles and a half southeast of the town, in the place called El Concejo, there is a rock over 300 feet high, cut off vertically. About one third the way up from the bottom is the entrance to a grotto, covered with brambles and about five feet high by nine feet wide. It has a number of caverns and arches, stalactites, and wonderful curiosities, etc., peculiar to caves generally.

The whole valley of the Arecibo is picturesque. Descending from the mountain of Utuado the entire course of the river presents itself to the view. On either side of its voluminous course are a number of streams forming beautiful cascades, and while delighting the traveller they also serve to irrigate the intermediate valleys which extend to the river. The latter becomes obstructed at the farther end and grows sluggish, its waters during freshets overflowing both banks and fertilizing the land for pastures, which are always covered with cattle, mules, and horses, the best on the island. In the centre of these meadows are seen the homes of the landowners, surrounded by leafy bananas, tall palms, and some sugar, coffee, and cotton plantations. The limits of each proprietor are marked by barriers of orange, lemon, and other trees which the fertile land produces in exquisite variety, the result being the most delightful and charming country imaginable.

Swinging around to a point on the northwest coast there opens up the magnificent bay of Aguadilla, capable of floating a navy, the town of the same name being the most picturesque of any in the island. It lies at the base of a very steep mountain covered with lemon and orange trees, palms, etc., and from a near-by ravine gushes out a spring of pure water of immense volume, which flows through the town to the sea. An antique church and an old fort add to the picturesqueness of the scene. It has about five thousand inhabitants, and five miles farther to the south, near the same large bay, is the town of Aguada, on the site where, tradition relates, Columbus first touched for water in 1493, and was so impressed with the beauty of the scene that he called it the " Rich Port," and the island " San Juan de Puerto Rico," or the Island of the Rich or Beautiful Port.

Due south lies the city of Mayagüez, with eleven thousand inhabitants, but twenty-eight thousand within its jurisdiction, the third city in im-

CITIES AND TOWNS OF THE COAST. 131

portance of the island, and one that exports vast quantities of sugar and coffee, pineapples and cocoanuts, and imports flour, etc., from the United States. It is the second port for coffee, its average annual export being about seventeen million pounds. The temperature is said rarely to exceed 90°, and the mountains are not far away, where the cool breezes always blow and from which pour down several rivers, notably the Mayagüez, from which in olden times much gold was obtained. A tramway connects this city with Aguadilla and other towns; it has no less than thirty-seven streets, three plazas, many modern handsome houses, fountains, and bridges. Its *vega*, or plain, is very fertile, and, like the valley of Arecibo, is dotted with planters' houses and the homes of the fruit-growers.

The market is the best on the island. It is constructed of iron and stone, covers an area of over fifteen hundred square yards, and cost seventy thousand *pesos*. About seven miles from Mayagüez, across a rough and mountainous country, is the sanctuary of Montserrate. This wild-looking place is visited by many who go there as pilgrims, and many legends are told concerning it.

The church is on top of a mountain. It is of masonry, quite capacious, and of agreeable aspect. From here is seen the most fertile and beautiful plain on the island, watered by the Juanajibos and

Boquerón rivers, and inclosed by high mountain ridges, which send forth multitudinous streams, the plain being bounded by the sea and having in it the towns of Cabo Rojo and San Germán.

Southeast of this town, and sixteen miles from San Germán, lies Yauco, one hundred and fifty feet above the sea, with a fine climate and good running water, under a range of high hills. It is connected by cart road with the port of Guanica, where there is a *playa*, or shore settlement of about one thousand people. This port was the initial point in the strategic plans of General Miles in his recent military occupation of Puerto Rico. As it has a "steep-to" shore, with a great depth of water, and there were no mines or fortifications, it was, of all the island ports, best suited for the purpose.

East of Yauco and connected with it by rail lies the city of Ponce, on the way to which is the town of Guayanilla, with six hundred inhabitants, situated near a seaport of the same name. Ponce, the chief city of the southern coast, the first in population, and second only to San Juan in commercial importance, was founded about 1600, and lies three miles from its *playa*, at the port, the spacious harbour of which will admit vessels of twenty-five feet draught. It became an American city, by surrender to General Miles, July 28, 1898.

CITIES AND TOWNS OF THE COAST. 133

The writer first visited Ponce in 1880, and then thought it the handsomest city of Puerto Rico, as it is doubtless the best equipped with hotels and comforts for the traveller. The latest statistics say of it:

A city of twenty-two thousand inhabitants, with a jurisdiction numbering forty-seven thousand. It is situated on the south coast of the island, on a plain, about two miles from the seaboard. It is the chief town of the judicial district of its name, and is seventy miles from San Juan. It is regularly built, the central part almost exclusively of brick houses and the suburbs of wood. It is the residence of the military commander, and the seat of an official chamber of commerce. There is an appellate criminal court, besides other courts; two churches, one Protestant, the only one in the island; two hospitals, besides the military hospital, a home of refuge for old and poor, two cemeteries, three asylums, several casinos, three theatres, a market, a municipal public library, three first-class hotels, three barracks, a park, gas works, a perfectly equipped fire department, a bank, thermal and natural baths, etc. A fine road leads to the port (Playa), where all the import and export trade is transacted. Playa has about five thousand inhabitants, and here are situated the custom house, the office of the captain of the port, and all the consular offices. The climate, on account of the sea breezes during the day and land breezes at night, is not oppressive, but very hot and dry; and as water for all purposes, including the fire department, is amply supplied by an aqueduct 4,442 yards long, it is said that the city of Ponce is perhaps one of the healthiest places in the island. There is a stage-road to San Juan, Mayagüez, Guayama, etc.; a railroad to Yauco, a post office, and a telegraph station.

It is believed that Ponce was founded in 1600; it was given the title of villa in 1848, and in 1877 that of city. Of its thirty-four streets, the best are Mayor, Salud, Villa, Vives, Marina, and Comercio. The best squares are Principal and Las Delicias, which are separated by the church of Nuestra Señora de Guadalupe. The church, as old as the town itself, was reconstructed between 1838 and 1847. It is eighty-six yards long by forty-three broad, and has two steeples, rich altars, and fine ornaments.

The Protestant church is of Gothic architecture, of galvanized iron outside and wood within, and was built in 1874.

The town hall, which also serves as a jail, is a good two-story building of masonry, and was finished in 1877. There are two barracks, one for infantry, with a capacity for seven hundred men, and another for cavalry. The former was constructed in 1849 and is two stories high, while the latter is a one-story structure belonging to the municipal council. The military hospital, of masonry, is situated on Castillo Street, and has a capacity for seventy patients.

The smallpox and pestilential hospitals are more simple and are situated outside the city limits.

The Albergue de Tricoche (hospital) was built with money left by Valentin Tricoche for this purpose, in 1863. It is in the northern part of the town, is built of masonry on the Doric order, with a porch supported by massive columns. It has a capacity for sixty persons.

The Damas Asylum is built of masonry, with an elegant porch, iron gate, and garden at its entrance. It is maintained by money left by various persons and by other charitable means, and will accommodate twelve men and twelve women, having besides four beds designed for sick seamen.

The theatre is called the Pearl, and it deserves this name, for it is the finest on the island. It has a sculptured porch, on the Byzantine order, with graceful columns. It is mostly built of iron and marble, and cost over seventy thousand *pesos*. It is fifty-two yards deep by twenty-nine wide. The inside is beautiful, the boxes and seats roomy, and nicely decorated. It may be, by a mechanical arrangement, converted into a dancing hall.

About a mile and an eighth northeast of the town are the Quintana thermal baths, in a building surrounded by pretty gardens. They are visited by sufferers from rheumatism and various other diseases.

There are three fairly good hotels in Ponce, the Français, the Inglaterra, and the Español, the first named being considered the best, as is consistent with the traditions of its nationality. The plaza is a pleasant gathering place, where, during Spanish occupation, a fine military band played between the hours of seven and nine at night, and the beauty and chivalry of the city assembled to enjoy themselves.

The next coast town of importance lies about fifty miles to the eastward of Ponce—Guayama, founded in 1736, containing about forty-five hundred inhabitants, and boasting one of the finest churches in Puerto Rico. Twelve miles west lies Salinas, inland from a good though small harbour, and five miles east is the port of Arroyo, which, though founded recently, already has a large export trade with the United States. The harbour of Arroyo, with its handsome town adjacent, was a landing place of our troops in their well-executed flank movement upon the mountain road from Ponce to San Juan, over a cart road leading from the coast to Cayey, thence northerly, cutting off the Spaniards from their base of supplies.

Arroyo is called one of the prettiest towns in the island, has a population of about twelve hundred, and sends to the United States annually some ten thousand hogsheads of sugar and five thousand of molasses, besides rum, etc. Near the port are

CITIES AND TOWNS OF THE COAST. 137

the wonderful caves of Aguas Buenas, three in number, called Oscura, Clara, and Ermita, and from the first named runs the river Caguïtas, which is a subterranean stream for about 1,200 feet. Iron is mined in the *barrio* of Yaurel, this district.

On the east coast the chief town is Humacao, on the river of that name, founded in 1793, and with about six thousand inhabitants. It is three miles from the coast, has a large and attractive plaza, a fine church, town house and jail, barracks, and hospital. This town suffered terribly in the hurricane of 1825.

Ten miles south of it lies Yabucoa, with four thousand population, half the entire number—as in the case of nearly all the towns and smaller cities—being black or coloured people.

Ten miles northeast of Humacao is the town of Naguabo, with two thousand people, which is of local importance from a tradition that it stands near or on the site where Columbus landed first in the island, coming from the eastward. A settlement that existed on the site of this town was attacked and destroyed by the Caribs in 1521.

Sixteen miles north lies Fajardo, in the extreme northeast of the island, and about two miles distant from its pretty port, which boasts a third-class light for the guidance of mariners. It contains about three thousand inhabitants, and drives a thriving trade with the United States in molasses and sugar, which are exchanged for shooks, lumber, and provisions. Dating from 1774, it is a place well known to seafaring men, and is said to have been the object of attack at one time, in 1824, by " Mr. Commodoro Porter." The sands of the Rio Fajardo are auriferous.

Having now arrived at the extreme northeast point of the island, from which we took our departure on this journey of inspection, we may be said to have " boxed the compass," even if we have not circumnavigated Puerto Rico. Before leaving this portion of the island, however, we should not fail to note the great pasture lands of the east and southeast, where vast herds of cattle and horses are reared, which form an important object of export to other islands of the Caribbean Sea.

XI.

INLAND TOWNS—ROUTES OF TRAVEL.

THE eastern division of Puerto Rico is less populous than the western, and also less conveniently situated for trade, lying as it does on the windward side of the island and offering little protection to shipping. Aside from the coast towns and cities already mentioned, the chief settlements, like Caguas, Cayey, etc., occupy the hilly region, in the midst of broad pastures and extensive coffee plantations.

Alphabetically arranged, the principal interior towns are as follows:

Adjuntas, with some 2,000 inhabitants, and 18,000 within its jurisdiction,* is situated about 15 miles from Ponce and has a post office and telegraph station. A popular mountain retreat, more than 2,400 feet above the coast level.

Aguada, already mentioned, with 2,500 population, and about 10,000 within the township, is

---

* The territory or section of which it is the most important settlement.

situated 5 miles from the port of Aguadilla, following the wagon road along the coast. In fact, though Aguadilla ("little Aguada") was formerly a smaller place than Aguada, as indicated by its name, it now surpasses it both in population and attractiveness.

Aguas Buenas is the centre of a township in which are some 8,000 people, about 5,000 coloured and 3,000 white. It lies 9 miles from Cayey and 24 from San Juan, with a wagon road to Caguas.

Aybonito, on the central highway from San Juan to Ponce, with post office and telegraph station, is a town of about 2,200 inhabitants, with 6,000 in its jurisdiction, two thirds white and one third coloured. It is also, from its elevated situation, nearly 3,000 feet above the sea, used as an acclimatization station, the climate being particularly fine, free from malarial germs, cool, and delightful.

Añasco, 6 miles from Mayagüez, has 4,000 inhabitants and about 13,000 within its jurisdiction, with post and telegraph station. It was in this district, in the Rio Guanroba, that the Indians drowned a Spaniard (about 1510) to ascertain beyond a doubt if he were mortal, before they rose in insurrection.

Barceloneta, on the north coast, with a railroad station and post office, has only 1,000 inhabitants, and 7,000 in the township.

Barranquitas, 28 miles distant from the nearest railroad station at Cantaño, is a town of but 700 people, with 7,000 in the jurisdiction, one third being coloured and two thirds white.

Barros, 31 miles from Ponce, is another small hamlet, though the chief town of a jurisdiction numbering about 13,000, with post and telegraph. The falls of Barros, in the hamlet of " Saltos," are very fine.

Bayamon, only 6 miles from San Juan, has 2,500 inhabitants, and about 15,000 within its jurisdiction; it is connected with the capital by rail, and has a post and telegraph station. Founded in 1772, it has the reputation of being a wealthy place, with several good streets, a town hall, jail, and barracks. The district produces sugar-cane, cattle, and tropical fruits. Caparra, the first settlement, now Pueblo Viejo, is in the Bayamon district.

Cabo Rojo, 8 miles from San Germán, has post and telegraph station, and something less than 3,000 inhabitants, with 17,000 in its jurisdiction, of which it is the principal town. There are extensive salt deposits in the Sierra de Peñones which have proved very profitable to their owners.

Caguas, with 4,000 inhabitants, has more coloured residents than white, and of the 15,000 people within its jurisdiction more than 8,000 of the former, and less than 7,000 of the latter. It has post and telegraph. There are hot springs in Caguïtas, this district, and a marble and limestone quarry in Cañaboncito.

Camuy, with about 1,000 inhabitants, has a railroad, telegraph, and post office, lies about 9 miles from Arecíbo, and contains 10,000 within its jurisdiction, most of whom are white.

Carolina, about 18 miles from San Juan, has post and telegraph and 5,000 inhabitants, with a jurisdiction of 10,000.

Cayey, with about 4,000 inhabitants, and some 14,000 within its jurisdiction, lies on the mountain road 37 miles from San Juan and 14 from Guayama, with post and telegraph station. Owing to its elevated situation, about 2,300 feet above sea level, it has a most agreeable climate, and is a favourite retreat for the coast dwellers during the heats of summer.

Ceiba, a town of 750 inhabitants, with jurisdiction of 4,000, lies 17 miles northeast of Humacao, has a post office and a wagon road to Fajardo and Naguabo.

Ciales, with 15,000 people within town and jurisdiction, lies in the mountains 19 miles from

Arecibo. It has a post station, but no telegraph, and from its isolation suffered severely at the hands of some Spanish troops soon after the evacuation of Ponce, when terrible outrages were committed upon its defenceless inhabitants.

Cidra (*Ciderville*), 6 miles from Cayey, has about 2,400 inhabitants, and within its jurisdiction a total of 8,000; has a post office.

Coamo has some 10,000 people within its jurisdiction, and about 2,200 in the hamlet, with post and telegraph station. It lies about 20 miles from Ponce, on the great highway to San Juan. It was reached by the American troops about the second week in August, 1898, when on their way from Ponce to Aybonito, and promptly capitulated. The town was founded in 1646, and the mineral medical waters of the Baños de Coamo have long been famous in the island and are visited by thousands.

Comeiro, municipal jurisdiction of about 6,600 people, has a post office and lies 17 miles from San Juan.

Corozal, town and jurisdiction of 11,500, 22 miles from San Juan, has a post office and telegraph station.

Dorado, with about 4,000 inhabitants, has a railroad, post and telegraph station, and is situated between 4 and 5 miles from San Juan.

Gurabo, a town of some 800 people, with a jurisdiction of 6,000, has post and telegraph; northwest of Humacao.

Hatillo, coast town, 6 miles west of Arecibo, with 400 inhabitants, in a jurisdiction of 9,000, has a post office.

Hato Grande, with about 2,000, jurisdiction of 12,600, 19 miles from Cayey, has post and telegraph.

Hormigueros, town and jurisdiction of 3,000, about 8 miles from San Germán, has post and telegraph stations.

Isabela, a municipal jurisdiction of 12,502 inhabitants, situated 10½ miles from Aguadilla, has good buildings of modern construction, and a post office. There is a wagon road to Aguadilla and Quebradillas.

Juana Diaz, a village and municipal jurisdiction of 21,032 inhabitants, is situated 8 miles from Ponce and 72 miles from San Juan. It has a post office and railroad station. The mineral waters of Catoni, in Amuelas, this district, are excellent in stomach troubles. Quarries of lime and gypsum are worked in Cintrona, and a curious cave exists in Guayabel.

Juncos, a municipal jurisdiction of 7,282 inhabitants, with a post office and telegraph station.

An iron mine is worked in the *barrio* of Ceiba-norte, in this jurisdiction.

Lares, a municipal jurisdiction of 17,020 inhabitants, of whom 15,005 are white, and 2,015 coloured. Población is the chief ward of the jurisdiction, with 1,575 inhabitants, situated 24 miles from Aguadilla. There is a wagon road to Aguadilla, Arecibo, and Mayagüez. There is a market every Sunday; there are casinos, a municipal library, and a post office. Situated 1,800 feet above sea level and has a delightful climate. In Callejones, this district, is a large cave known as the Pajita.

Las Marias, a town of 750 inhabitants, with a jurisdiction numbering 9,700, situated 15½ miles from Mayagüez, has two theatres and two casinos. The nearest railroad station is in Naranjales, at a distance of 6 miles. There is a post office and telegraph station.

Loiza, a town of 907 inhabitants, chief town of a jurisdiction of 9,561, is situated 19 miles from San Juan. The nearest railroad station is Rio Piedras, 19 miles distant. It has a post office. Near Loiza exists a large cave known as the Indian Cavern, and a wonderful waterfall.

Luquillo, a town of 1,560 inhabitants, with a jurisdiction numbering 6,893, is situated 31 miles from Humacao. Gold exists in the sands of its rivers. The nearest railroad station is Carolina, 19 miles distant. Has a post office. It is said that a rich gold mine was formerly worked in the *barrio* of Mameyes, this district, but a furious hurricane obliterated all traces of it many years ago.

Manati, a town and jurisdiction of 11,967 inhabitants, is situated 17 miles from Arecibo. There is a railroad station, a post office, and a telegraph station. There is a spacious cavern near the town called Swallow Cave.

Maricao, a municipal jurisdiction of 8,000 inhabitants, is situated $9\frac{1}{2}$ miles from San Germán and $15\frac{1}{2}$ from Mayagüez, with a wagon road to Mayagüez and Las Marias. It lies about 1,500 feet above the sea, and there is, or was, an iron mine within the limits of the township.

Maunabo, a town of 903 inhabitants, of whom 346 are white and 567 coloured. It is the chief town of a jurisdiction of 5,689 inhabitants—1,495 white and 4,194 coloured. It is situated 24 miles from Guayama, with a post office and telegraph station.

Moco, a village of 1,034 inhabitants, with a jurisdiction numbering 11,084, is situated $4\frac{1}{2}$ miles from the station of Aguadilla, with which it is connected by a wagon road. Has a post office.

INLAND TOWNS—ROUTES OF TRAVEL. 147

Morovis, a town of 619 inhabitants, with a jurisdiction numbering 8,234, is situated 32 miles from Arecibo, and has a post office.

Naranjito, a municipal jurisdiction of 5,825 inhabitants, is situated 21 miles from San Juan.

Patillas, a municipal jurisdiction of 10,553 inhabitants, is situated 62 miles from Guayama. It has a post office. Rock crystals in masses are found in the hills of Mala Pascua, this district.

Peñuelas, a town of 859 inhabitants, with a jurisdiction numbering 10,623, is situated 10 miles from Ponce.

Piedras, a town of 1,200 inhabitants, of whom 900 are white and 300 coloured. It is the chief town of a jurisdiction of 8,545 inhabitants—5,698 white and 2,847 coloured. It is situated $3\frac{2}{3}$ miles from Humacao, on the highway from San Juan to Humacao. Has a post office. In the *barrio* of Collares, this jurisdiction, iron is mined.

Quebradillas, a town of 1,055 inhabitants—868 white and 187 coloured. Chief town of a jurisdiction of 5,899 inhabitants, of whom 3,520 are white and 379 coloured. It is situated $17\frac{1}{2}$ miles from Aguadilla. Has a post office.

Rincón, a town of 300 inhabitants, with a jurisdiction numbering 5,817, is situated 15 miles from Mayagüez. It has a railroad station and a post office.

148 PUERTO RICO AND ITS RESOURCES.

Rio Grande, a town of 695 inhabitants, of whom 220 are white and 475 coloured. It is the chief town of a jurisdiction of 6,170 inhabitants, 2,444 of whom are white and 3,726 coloured. The town has 8 wards. It is situated 25 miles from San Juan. The nearest railroad station is Luquillo, 27 kilometres distant, and it has a post office.

Rio Piedras, a town of 1,054 inhabitants—581 white and 473 coloured. It is the chief town of a jurisdiction of 9,010 inhabitants, of whom 3,482 are white and 5,528 coloured. It is situated 7 miles from San Juan, with which it is connected by a railroad. It has a theatre and a *casa de recreo*, or country house, for the governors of the province. There is a post office and telegraph station.

Sabana Grande, a municipal jurisdiction of 9,587 inhabitants, is situated 18 miles from Mayagüez, on the highway from Mayagüez to Ponce, with a post office.

Within this district, at Rincón, is a cascade well worth a visit, and in the *barrio* of Rayo a spring, the waters of which are said to be efficacious in several diseases.

Salinas, a town of 655 inhabitants, with a jurisdiction numbering 4,104 inhabitants, is situated 22 miles from Cayey and 12 from Guayama. It has a good harbour a short distance from town. The salt deposits which give this district its name—Salinas—are found in the *barrio* of Aguirre.

San Germán, a city of 8,000 inhabitants, with a jurisdiction numbering 30,600, is situated 115 miles from San Juan. It has three fine market places, a charity hospital, a seminary, good school buildings, theatre, casino, etc. There is a railroad in construction, and a post office and telegraph station.

It is situated on a long, uneven hill, at the foot of which lies the beautiful valley of the Juanajibos and Boquerón rivers, which is made a beautiful garden by the orange, lemon, and tamarind trees, and various other plants growing here. Coffee, cotton, and cane are also raised.

The town was founded in 1511 by Captain Miguel Toro, and has enjoyed the title of city since 1877. Its principal streets are Luna and Comercio. Its chief plaza is square and large in size, with a church of ancient construction. There are two hospitals—one for men and one for women. The town hall is a good building, of masonry, two stories high, with a clock tower.

San Sebastian, a town of 1,200 inhabitants, with a jurisdiction numbering 16,000, is situated 14 miles from Aguadilla; has a post office and telegraph station. Two great caves are found in this district, at Guajataca and Enea, a waterfall called the Salto de Collazo, and warm springs at Pozas.

Santa Isabel, a municipal jurisdiction of 3,200 inhabitants, is situated 63 miles from San Juan and 16 miles from Ponce; has a post office and telegraph station.

San Turce, the fifth district from the capital, with 3,640 inhabitants, is situated 3 miles from San Juan.

Toa Alta, a town of 1,100 inhabitants, with a jurisdiction numbering 7,821, is situated 15½ miles from San Juan; there is a second-class wagon road and a post office.

Toa Baja, a municipal jurisdiction of 3,481 inhabitants, is situated 10½ miles from San Juan; has a post office.

Trujillo Alto, a town of 1,800 inhabitants, with a jurisdiction numbering 4,072, is situated 15 miles from San Juan. The nearest railroad station is Rio Piedras, 7½ miles distant; has a post office.

Utuado, a town of 3,738 inhabitants, of whom 2,123 are white and 1,615 coloured, is the chief town of a jurisdiction of 30,045 inhabitants, 22,-757 of whom are white. It is situated 56 miles from San Juan and 14 miles from Arecibo, with a wagon road to the capital. There is a post office and a telegraph station. An excellent situation, 1,500 feet above the sea.

In the Utuado district are several fine cascades, the Salto de Morones, Saltillos, and Canalizos; there is a cave near Caguana called the Cavern of the Dead, because of the Indian skeletons which were found there many years ago.

Vega Alta, a town of 985 inhabitants, of whom 225 are white and 760 coloured, is the chief town of a jurisdiction of 5,420 inhabitants—situated 22 miles from San Juan. The nearest railroad station is that of Vega Baja, 12½ miles distant, with a first-class wagon road. There is a post office.

Villa de la Vega Baja, a village of 2,531 inhabitants, chief town of the judicial district of its name, with municipal jurisdiction of 10,650 inhabitants, is situated 23½ miles from San Juan. There is a railroad, a post office, and a telegraph station.

Its church, which forms one of the façades fronting on the beautiful plaza, is in its proportions and general appearance one of the finest in the island. Its two towers are elegant, one containing a bell and the other the public clock. Opposite the church is the town hall, a fine building of rubble masonry of one story, but large enough to hold, besides the municipal offices, the jail and police station. The aspect of the square and of the whole village is very agreeable.

While a system of communication exists along the coast, and, in the words of M. Reclus, " in respect to its internal communications Puerto Rico is a model West Indian island," yet the only really excellent road of any length is that between San Juan and Ponce. Though, as the author just quoted observes, "all the towns are connected by highways which develop around the periphery of the quadrilateral a second quadrilateral, all the sides of which are united at intervals by transverse routes," yet most of the lateral and transverse roads are little more than trails or horse paths, almost if not quite impassable in rainy weather, without bridges, and not of sufficient width for carriages.

For interior communication there are only a few local roads or paths. They are usually two yards in width, made by the various owners, and can not be well travelled in rainy weather. They are more properly horse and mule trails, and oblige people to go in single file. In late years much has been attempted to improve the highways connecting the principal cities, and more has been accomplished than in most Spanish colonies. There is a good made road connecting Ponce on the southern coast with San Juan, the capital. Other good roads

Native hut, country district.

INLAND TOWNS—ROUTES OF TRAVEL. 153

also extend for a short distance along the north coast and along the south coast. The road from Guayama is also said to be a passably good one.

There are in the island about one hundred and fifty miles of excellent road, and this is all that receives any attention, transportation being effected elsewhere on horseback. In the construction of a road level foundation is sought, and on this is put a heavy layer of crushed rock and brick, which, after having been well packed and rounded, is covered with a layer of earth. This is well packed also, and upon the whole is spread a layer of ground limestone, which is pressed and rolled until it forms almost a glossy surface. This makes an excellent road here, where the climate is such that it does not affect it, and when there is no heavy traffic; but these conditions being changed, the road, it is thought, would not stand so well.

From Palo Seco, situated about a mile and a half from the capital, on the opposite side of the bay, a carriage road, perfectly level, has been constructed for a distance of twenty-two leagues to the town of Aguadilla on the west coast, passing through the towns of Vega Baja, Manatí, Arecibo, Hatillo, Camuy, and Isabella. This road has been carried for several leagues over swampy lands, which are intersected by deep drains to carry off the water.

The road from Aguadilla to Mayagüez is in some parts very good, in other parts only fair. From Aguadilla to Aguada, a distance of a league, the road is excellent and level. From thence to Mayagüez, through the village of Rincón and the town of Añasco, the road is generally good, but on the seashore it is sometimes interrupted by shelving rocks. Across the valley of Añasco the road is carried through a boggy tract, with bridges over several deep creeks of fresh water. From thence to the large commercial town of Mayagüez the road is uneven and requires some improvement. But the roads from Mayagüez and Ponce to their respective ports on the seashore can not be surpassed by any in Europe. They are made in a most substantial manner, and their convex form is well adapted to preserve them from the destruction caused by the heavy rains of the climate. These roads have been made over tracts of swampy ground to the seacoast, but with little and timely repair they will last forever.

A road, which may be called a carriage road, has been made from Ponce to the village of Adjuntas, situated five leagues in the interior of the mountains. The road along the coast, from Ponce to Guayama, is fairly good; from thence to Patillas there is an excellent carriage road for a distance of three leagues; from the latter place to the coast is a highroad well constructed. From Patillas to Fajardo, on the eastern coast, passing through the towns of Maimavo, Yubacao, Humacao, and Naguabo, the roads are not calculated for wheel vehicles, in consequence of being obliged to ascend and descend several steep hills. That which crosses the mountain of Mala Pascua, dividing the north and east coasts, is a good and solid road, upon which a person on horseback may travel with great ease and safety. The road crossing the valley of Yubacao, which consists of a soft and humid soil, requires more attention than that crossing the mountain at Mala Pascua, which has a fine, sandy soil.

From Fajardo to the capital, through the towns of Luquillo, Loisa, and Rio Piedras, the road is tolerably good for persons on horseback as far as Rio Piedras, and from thence to the city of San Juan, a distance of two leagues, is an excellent carriage road, made by the order and under the inspection of the captain-general, part of it through a mangrove swamp. Over the river Loisa is a handsome bridge, and on the road near Rio Piedras is a handsome stone one over a deep rivulet.

One of the best roads in the island extends from the town of Papino, situated in the mountains, to the town of Aguadilla on the coast, distant five leagues and a half, through the village of La Moca, a distance of three leagues from the latter place. It is crossed by ten deep mountain rivulets, formerly impassable, but over which solid bridges have now been built, with side railings. In the mountainous district within the circumference of a few leagues no less than forty-seven bridges have been built to facilitate the communication between one place and the other.

The following are the roads of six metres width, four and a half in centre of pounded stone. They have iron bridges and are in good shape for travel all the year:

(1) *San Juan to the Shore near Ponce.*—From San Juan to Ponce the central road is exactly 134 kilometres. Distances along the line are: Rio Piedras, 11; Caguas, 25; to Cayei, 24; Aybonito, 20; Coamo, 18; Juana Díaz, 20; to Ponce, 13; and to the shore, 3. Exact.

(2) *San Juan to Bayamon.*—By ferry fifteen minutes to Cataño, and from there by road to Bayamon 10 kilometres. This passes alongside the railway.

(3) Rio Piedras to Mameyes, 36 kilometres: from Rio Piedras to Carolina, 12; to Rio Grande, 19; to Mameyes, 5.

(4) Cayei to Arroyo, 35 kilometres; from Cayei to Guayama, 25; to Arroyo, 8; from San Juan to Arroyo, via Cayei, is 95 kilometres.

(5) Ponce to Adjuntas, 32 kilometres.

(6) San Germán to Añasco, 33 kilometres; from San Germán to Mayagüez, 21 kilometres; Mayagüez to Añasco, 12; Mayagüez to Hormigueros, 11; Mayagüez to Cabo Rojo, 18; Mayagüez to Las Marias, 23; Mayagüez to Maricao, 35; Hormigueros, to San Germán, 14. Near Mayagüez the roads are best. There are good roads in all directions.

(7) Aguadilla to San Sebastian, 18.

(8) Arecibo to Utuado, 33.

INLAND TOWNS—ROUTES OF TRAVEL.

Table of Distances, in Miles, between Principal Places.

Adjuntas.												
44	Aguadilla.											
24	30	Arecibo.										
60	36	66	Bayamon.									
48	130	94	28	Cayey.								
27	76	40	42	16	Coamo.							
98	104	74	38	45	61	Fajardo.						
54	140	104	38	14	26	46	Guayama.					
64	102	72	33	29	44	16	29	Humacao.				
26	17	32	69	76	60	106	78	102	Mayagüez.			
16	54	40	60	35	19	80	38	63	36	Ponce.		
25	26	33	99	63	47	108	66	91	8	28	San Germán.	
66	81	50	6	37	48	36	49	42	102	70	115	San Juan de Puerto Rico.
44	20	20	17	45	24	56	44	50	54	40	54	23	Vega Baja.
18	38	38	104	52	36	97	54	79	22	16	15	82	58	Yauco.

XII.

GOVERNMENT AND PEOPLE.

UNDER Spanish rule Puerto Rico was governed as a province of Spain, rather than as a colony. All authority was centralized in the person of a viceroy, who, as governor and captain-general, was civil ruler and military commander of the forces. In each military district resided an officer in command of an armed force, and each town or city was presided over by its *alcalde*, or mayor, appointed by the central power. Under the same regulations as prevail in Spain, the provincial deputation was elected by popular suffrage, which, however, was less a franchise than a farce! The regular peace garrison of the island was about three thousand men, and the annual expenses usually absorbed the revenues.

The island was divided territorially into the capital and seven departments. The first (1) was the territorial division of Bayamon, in the northeast, the agricultural features of which are sugar-cane, pasturage, fine woods in the forests, some coffee, and tropical fruits. (2) Arecibo, on the north coast, producing sugar-cane, tobacco, coffee, and fine cattle. (3) Aguadilla, thoroughly tropical in its resources of coffee, sugar, cocoanuts, and all other tropic fruits. (4) Mayagüez, same as the last named. (5) Ponce, sugar, coffee, etc. (6) Guayama, grazing, sugar-cane, coffee in the hills. (7) Humacao, with sugar-cane, some coffee, and vast areas of pasturage.

The prosperity of Puerto Rico, says the author of Nouvelle Géographie Universelle, is shown as much in its general material progress as in its increased population. Since the middle of the last century the social condition of the inhabitants has undergone a complete change. At that time the peasantry dwelt in rude hovels without shutters or doors, and their only utensils were calabashes; an empty bottle was considered worthy of being handed down as an heirloom to the favourite son! . . . During this century the yield of coffee, sugar, tobacco, and to a less extent honey and wax, have enriched the island, which now possesses the means of purchasing all the wares of the civilized world. Most of the exchange is carried on with the United States, whence come corn, flour, salt fish, meats, and lumber, in return for sugar, coffee, molasses, etc. Nearly all the sea-borne traffic is under foreign flags, the islanders having but little taste for a seafaring life. . . . In 1765 the population numbered but forty-five thousand (?), now exceeds eight hundred thousand, and has doubled itself on an average every thirty years—a rate almost as rapid as that of the French Canadians. This is due mainly to the fertility of the soil and to the large immigrations from Spanish-American colonies during the wars for independence, from 1810 to 1825. . . . It is one of the few countries in tropical America where the whites outnumber the black and coloured people, and the males exceed the females. It is remarkable to find the European race on the whole increasing more rapidly than the African, in a climate certainly more favourable to the latter!

While we can not arbitrarily differentiate the natives of this island from other Hispano-Americans, still they have their peculiarities. According to the latest available statistics, there is a population here of eight hundred and thirteen thousand, of which less than half, or about three hundred and twenty-six thousand, are of mixed blood or coloured. The racial type, as well as the language, is Spanish, and education has not received here any greater attention than in the mother country, scarcely more than one seventh being able to read and write. There are some good schools, as well as colleges of low grade, while every district has, or is supposed to have, its school of primary instruction. There will doubtless be a great demand in the very near future for teachers who can speak, read, and write Spanish as well as English—that is, if we are to keep pace with our traditions and seek to implant in the minds of these insular colonists of ours a knowledge of our institutions.

There were, at the time the island became an American possession, some five hundred primary schools and numerous of secondary and higher grade, but no institution for the "higher education."

"The Puertoriqueños," wrote an author of the last century, "are well proportioned and delicately organized, yet at the same time they lack vigour; are slow and indolent, yet possess vivid imaginations; are vain and inconstant, yet hospitable to strangers and most ardent lovers of liberty." He then describes the *Cheutos*, as the descendants of the Majorcan Jews are called; the *Gibaros*, or Indio-Spanish *mestizos*, etc., and says of them: "From this variety of mixture has resulted a character that is equivocal and ambiguous, but peculiarly Puertoriqueñian. The heat of the climate has made them indolent, to which end also the fertility of the soil has conduced, and the solitary life of the country residents has rendered them rather morose."

It is well known that the Latin peoples do not share in the aversion felt by the Teutons and Anglo-Saxons for the races that have complexions more deeply dyed than theirs. French affiliation with aboriginal peoples is a matter of notoriety; but between the French and the Spanish is this difference: that while the former were spontaneous in their expressions of affection for the red and black and copper-coloured inhabitants of lands they conquered, the latter courted them only with ulterior motive. The result is shown in the mixed peoples, the product of amalgamation with either nationality, for while the French resultant is agile, witty, laughter-loving, and affectionate, the Spanish is more often morose and treacherous.

Now, to specialize from these generalizations: The Spaniards in Puerto Rico and other West Indian islands did not so thoroughly eliminate the aborigines that no traces remain of Indian blood in the veins of the present inhabitants. In other words, there are many half-breeds, or mixed people —*mestizos* and *mestizas*—who can trace connections, more or less remote and uncontaminated, with the ancient race of Puerto Rico.

Add to these the Africans, the Majorcan Jews, and the Canary Islanders, who have been brought here at one time or another, and the various half-

GOVERNMENT AND PEOPLE. 163

castes resulting from the mingling of these bloods with the Spanish, and one may not wonder that of the total population of Puerto Rico pretty nearly one half is something else than Castilian, pure and undefiled.

Slavery was abolished thirty years ago, but during the time it flourished many thousands were imported from Africa and many other thousands born in the island of African blood, so that the majority of people other than of Spanish birth can point to the Dark Continent as the home of their ancestors.

Computing the population at eight hundred thousand, in round numbers, not more than half of that number, or say four hundred thousand, are of Spanish ancestry, and the other half composed mainly of mixed bloods. This statement is not made as a matter of reproach, but of fact. If the Spaniard chose to consort with the tawny beauty of the forest and raise a brood of semi-savage children, that was surely his business, and no reproach to him so long as he remained faithful to his family. But the records, so far as they are accessible, do not show a fidelity to the marital vow on the part of the man that is at all edifying. Perhaps the climate may have been to blame, for where children may disport themselves in the garb invented and worn by the sartorial artists of Eden, crave no greater excitement than a cock-fight and no greater variety of food than a raw banana or boiled yam, the tendency is toward Nature's way!

There may not have been so striking examples of aboriginal atavism as are seen across the channel in Haiti, where the African sorcery has become paramount and serpent worship is still practised, because the Spanish parent was the stronger and held the offspring to the paternal type. There are some who think it would have been better if the aboriginal type had been preserved and continued, especially as the Spaniard who came here to conquer new lands did not come from any better motives than that of acquiring wealth, nor from any other desire than to gratify his lust for gold and for blood. He rarely came as a colonist, in the sense that the Anglo-Saxon regarded the settling of strange countries.

Doubtless, if the Spaniard had found all he expected here, the race inhabiting these islands to-day would be the most cruel on the face of the earth. If the gold, the rich mines, the opportunities for the enslavement of his fellow men which were afforded in the first century of his settling here—if these had continued, with their consequent license for unbridled passions, for the perpetuation of unmitigated cruelties, such as stain the page of history wherever Spain has gone for conquest—the people of Puerto Rico would hardly be fit subjects for acquisition by the United States.

But poverty is the great leveller. It is here as it is in Spain. While the Spanish Government is a hideous thing—a survival of the times of Charles I and Philip II, smacking of the Inquisition and *autos da fé*—the Spanish common people are at heart honest, lovable, and trustworthy. They have been subjected to oppression in all its forms, until at last they know of no other life than that of poverty, with its grinding toil, its deprivations. So with the common people—and they predominate here—of Puerto Rico. They will welcome any change that brings them a new opportunity. Not that they understand what it may be or how to avail themselves of it when it comes; but they are intelligent enough to know that nothing could be worse than the life they lead now.

But while the opening of the island to a redevelopment will mean the releasing of the common people from a hidebound despotism, it is by no means certain that there will be great opportunities for the acquisition of wealth, either through the exploitation of mineral or agricultural resources, by immigrants from the United States.

The conditions that have prevailed for centuries can not be changed in a day; the lands to which titles have been held for hundreds of years can not be alienated in a short time; even the lands that may fall to our Government by right of conquest will have to remain inaccessible for some time. But that there are mineral resources worth exploiting, tracts well worth purchase for development by means of modern agricultural operations—coffee lands in the hills and sugar lands along the coast —we have every reason to believe.

While the better classes are mainly engaged in business and are of Spanish origin, most of the poorer are resident in the country, or, what is far worse, living from hand-to-mouth in the towns and cities. It seems incredible that an island thirty-six hundred miles in area, much of it arable land, capable of producing every variety of fruit and vegetable known to the tropics, should yet contain a population a large proportion of which is poverty-stricken. Yet such is the case, and whether a better government will change the conditions so radically that all will be improved in means, and also afford an opening for enterprising Americans, remains to be seen.

It is not strange that poverty exists in the North, where a long winter prevents the poor from

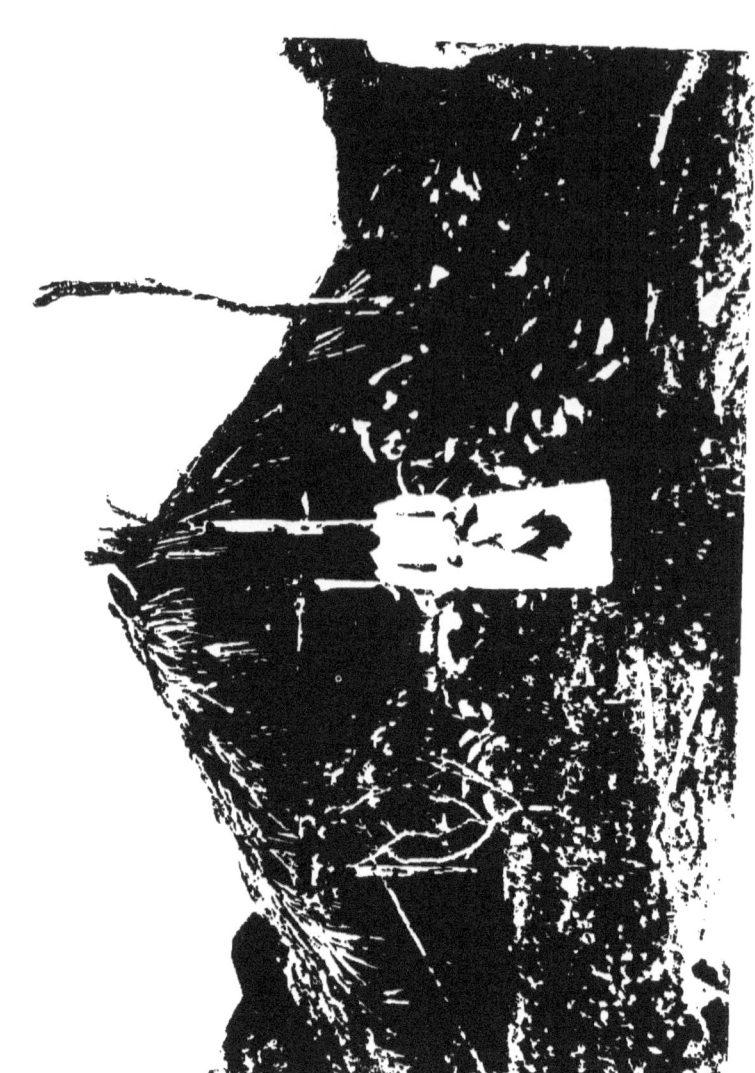

A shelter of palm leaves.

raising even the necessaries of existence; but in a land where the sun always shines, where it is never impossible to plant and sow, to harvest and gather fruit—to find people there without the means for supporting life, and in the country districts at that, seems inexplicable. The reason for this condition lies not on the surface of things, but down in the primitive foundations of society.

The children, as has been intimated, white, black, and coloured of both sexes, disport themselves " in their complexions " merely, varied by such additions of dirt as they may receive while at play, and which is not always removed at night. They are naturally cleanly, as are most dwellers in tropical countries, because the bath is always refreshing, and to paddle in cool streams (if they may be found) and beneath overarching tree-ferns and bananas is pleasanter than rolling in the dirt. But cleanliness is only a relative term, depending upon the surroundings. In the large towns and cities, where opportunities for bathing are infrequent, the youngsters are not so inviting in appearance as in the country districts, along the coast, or where, in fact, pools and streams are available.

The country people live as nearly in a state of nature as they can and as the laws will allow, simply because a state of nature fits them best and is comfortable. The children reluctantly don the garb of civilization at or near the age of ten or twelve, and then only after many and tearful protestations. In their innocence, they see no harm in going naked; they are certainly free from the pruriency which attends the wearing of clothes; their forms are symmetrical, their health is generally good. But for the existence of fevers and of such noxious insects as centipeds, tarantulas, scorpions, etc., child life in the tropics would be without any alloy of unhappiness.

It is in the market places that the common people most assemble and may be studied to the best advantage. There, as well as in the shops, it will be seen that their transactions are of a very humble character, chiefly measured in small change and not in dollars. Each vender has a space assigned, within which are piled small heaps of fruits or vegetables that he or she has brought from the country, and not infrequently a fighting cock is tied to the leg of the little stool on which the vender is sitting.

Making love, of course, goes on all the time, for the creole nature is soft and languishing, complaisant, easily tickled by compliment, and prone to hanker after the "forbidden fruit." Scratch a Puerto Rican and you find a Spaniard underneath the skin, so the language and home customs of Spain prevail here, as in Cuba. The ladies of the upper classes are strictly secluded and have little freedom, yet entrance into society here is more easily attained than in Spain or in Cuba. That the ladies are charming, goes without saying. They differ from the Havanese as the gentlewomen of New York and Newport differ from their sisters in the country. They are insular, even provincial perhaps, but they possess charming traits of character, gentle manners and speech, goodness of heart, and unaffected frankness with their friends. Their acquaintance is an easier matter of accomplishment than that of the Havana ladies; still they are surrounded with the same safeguards that hedge about the others, and which the ardent young men deem so superfluous.

To one who has had the pleasure of meeting them at home and of being introduced into their society by a mutual friend, the remembrance of their graciousness seems like a bit of good fortune, that rarely falls to the lot of the West Indian traveller.

Those of gentle birth and breeding are sweet and flower-like, with a bright alertness peculiar to the Latin woman transplanted to American soil and climate. Their glances are swift and meaning, their great black eyes capable of seeming quite full of expression; their features are not always classically regular, but usually attractive. They are petite of form and have small hands and feet, dress in the latest style from Paris (the "latest" being usually two years old by the time it reaches Puerto Rico), and, in a word, are thoroughly feminine. It is this charm of femininity that makes the creole, whether French or Spanish, so potent with man. It was a creole, it will be remembered —Josephine, a native of Martinique—who captivated and ruled Napoleon. She ruled him, that is, in all matters domestic and within her ken and comprehension; her limitations were those of her sex, her weapons tact and a persuasive charm of graciousness.

One is continually reminded, in this island, of the Oriental ancestry of its Spanish inhabitants, particularly by their dwellings, with open central courts, or *patios*, flat roofs, or *azoteas*, and the fountains plashing their waters on surrounding flowers. These are the houses of the better classes, their massive stone walls maintaining a seclusion, and their interiors steeped in an air of mystery as deep as that enveloping the harem of any Turk of Cairo or Constantinople. The characteristics of the family also are Oriental, bearing the impress of the Arabs who conquered Spain a thousand years and more ago, and who lived seven long centuries in the Iberian peninsula. The Puerto Rican home life, in fact, differs in no important particular from that of Spain and Mexico, Havana and Madrid, but it is very difficult for the stranger to obtain even a glimpse of the Hispano-American *gynæceum*. In the writer's experience it was primarily accomplished by engaging quarters in the family of an indigent Don who had seen better days. It was not a boarding house he kept; perish the thought! but a *casa de huespedes*, and at his table assembled people of the highest quality—that is, *solteros*, or bachelors, editors of papers, *attachés* at the captain-general's palace, and military men.

The taking of a stranger with one to call on a friend in his home is considered at least a breach of privilege; however, there was a bright young lady at the house, of American parentage, who was the object of a certain Spanish gentleman's adoration, and this Spaniard had a pretty cousin, a sweet young lady, who was not enamoured of any one in particular, and who kindly consented to accompany her male relative in his frequent calls at the *casa de huespedes*, for appearance's sake. Thus, if the reader can make out from this very involved explanation that the little cousin, though exceedingly interesting, was yet considered by the lovers as somewhat in the way, it may be understood how it came about that she and the writer occupied the balcony, while the twain held *tête-à-tête* in the parlour.

A disinterested act like this brought its own reward, for from his fair interlocutrice the writer obtained a deal of information not set down in the books, and eventually his introduction into the home of her family. Our conversations sometimes turned quite easily on love, and the query naturally arose, whether there were really any differences in the manner of love making as practised by our respective nationalities.

The writer made the discovery—perhaps not an original one—that the Spanish-American lover, like his Saxon sympathizer, frequently drops into poesy as a means of relieving the pressure on his overburdened heart. The stock poetry of lovers is about the same in both languages, English and Spanish, differing mainly in having a different tag on it, one quoting Byron or Tom Moore, perchance, and the other—well, some author of celebrity in España. Sometimes, like his fellow-sufferer in this country, he strives to be original, and even his prose takes a tinge of poetry, as shown by this example extracted from a young lady's album of verse and sentiment:

Angel of light! Flower born in heaven and watered by angels' tears! Pardon me that I even attempt to utter with these profane lips thy sacred name! It is not a song only that I would fain offer thy delicate ears, but a blessing, a benediction; a feeble effort, it is true, but as pure as thy beauty, as enthusiastic as the soul of youth, since to sing thy manifold graces worthily, I confess, it would be necessary to hire a choir of angels and a heavenly harp!

It is not possible for a mere mortal, who has only received from on high a heart receptive, a soul responsive, to bask in the flame of thy beauty without being consumed with admiration, with veneration, and yet with sadness!

And so on, until the courtship is completed and wedding bells, perhaps, ring out the knell of poesy and passion.

Each country has its type of beauty, each type is the theme of enthusiastic writers—has been from time immemorial. The type here is also that of Spain, the mother country. Brunettes prevail and blondes are a rarity. The large eyes, black as night; the peachblow complexion; hair abundant, dark and glossy as a raven's wing; gracefully moulded, voluptuous form—these attributes of Spanish beauty have not changed during all the three hundred years of Spanish domination.

The ladies do not veil their faces, to be sure, like the Oriental odalisques, though they protect them with powder, unsparingly and unblushingly applied. Visit any school in the island and you will find teacher and scholar alike wearing this mask of beauty. Even the pupils of the art schools, as well as the workwomen in the cigar shops, use the powdery protection against the sun's rays. On every easel in the art academy and on the bench by the side of every woman engaged in rolling cigarette or cigar lies a little box of powder and a rabbit's foot. There is nothing unusual in this public use of the article, since its application is so universal, through long custom, and all ladies regard it as an indispensable adjunct of the toilet, and absolutely necessary to make them attractive; which is, or should be, their highest ambition.

The range of household occupations is not great, consisting chiefly of embroidery and needlework. In the higher vocations few of them are employed, though now and then one attains to local distinction in sculpture or painting. Prohibited pleasures are many, and those in which women may indulge very few -indeed.

To conclude this chapter with a Spanish writer's opinion of the *bello sexo* of the island: " The fair sex are sweet and amiable, faithful as wives, loving as sisters, sweethearts, and daughters, ornaments to any society in the world, tasteful in dress, tactful in conversation, graceful in deportment, and extremely elegant in their carriage. In truth, visitors from Old Spain have often remarked their resemblance to the beautiful *doncellas* of Cadiz, who indeed are world famous for their beauty, grace, and loveliness!"

All the islanders speak Spanish, of course, are governed by Spanish laws, profess the Roman Catholic religion, and have Spanish habitudes. Owing to the comparative density of population in the country districts, most of the people are poor, and extremely poor at that. According to the author of a book published in Spain, called La Cuestion de Puerto Rico, the density of population is most extraordinary, with about 1,744 inhabitants to every square (Spanish) league, while in Cuba it is only 376. The writer argues from this the eventual prosperity of the greater number, as there will be no opportunity for such vast holdings as in Cuba, with their consequent development of a landed class. Twenty years ago the number of individual proprietors here was more than fifty-five thousand, while in Cuba at the same time, with double the population, they did not exceed twenty-eight thousand.

This subject has an important aspect at present, when so many Americans doubtless cherish the hope of acquiring some holding or other in our new possessions. But while it is well known that the island is already well inhabited, ranking fourth or fifth only from the most densely populated country in the world, yet it is the opinion of those acquainted with Puerto Rico and its possibilities that it can safely hold two hundred thousand more without inconvenience, or at least a round million of inhabitants.

XIII.

FOODS, DRINKS, DIVERSIONS, ETC.

Our Jack tars hold it as an axiom that there is no Sabbath in four-fathom waters, nor in foreign countries, where that holy day is mainly given over to amusements. That is, Jack gives himself the benefit of the doubt, when the religious forms and ceremonies are dubious, and on the sacred day of the seven joins the throng and follows the crowd, which in Cuba and Puerto Rico betakes itself to the cockpit and the bull ring—in the vernacular, the *valla de gallos* and the *corrida de toros*.

Had you crossed, perchance, the main plaza of San Juan de Puerto Rico almost any Sunday morning between the hours of eight and nine, before the late change of ownership, you might have heard a loud whirring and clacking from the corridor of an ancient structure. If you had investigated, you would have discovered two perspiring black boys turning a crank attached to an immense wooden globe, within which, as it is hollow, were the tickets for the current lottery of the municipality. After the tickets have been thoroughly stirred up the motion ceases and one of the "motors," having been blindfolded, thrusts in a hand and extracts a bit of pasteboard. Then the wooden sphere is whirled around again and the several processes are repeated until all the lucky numbers have been taken from this queer and primitive receptacle.

This is merely preliminary to the festivities of the day, and after all the good Cubanos and Puerto Riquenos have been to church, or during the latter half of the afternoon, they hie themselves to the bull ring or the cockpit, which are usually in the suburbs of the city. Ladies are countenanced at the former, but only the sterner sex may indulge in the recreations of the latter.

The largest *valla de gallos* of Puerto Rico is probably that of San Juan, the capital of the island, and is situated just without the city walls, in the Marina beneath the frowning harbour-front of the great fortress. It is not an ambitious structure architecturally, being merely a rough wall of mason-work, topped by a roof of corrugated iron, inclosing a circular arena covered with sawdust. If you are not acquainted with the locality and wish to ascertain where the "pit" is situated, you have only to do what you would be likely to in our country in order to find the whereabouts of the

Game cocks on the sidewalk, San Juan.

most popular preacher—follow the crowd! They say, in truth, that in most places in Puerto Rico, especially in the small towns, you have only to follow the priest, who, as soon as services are over, tucks up his cassock, whips a favourite cock under his arm, and "streaks it" for the arena!

A fee of twenty-five cents gives general admission, but an additional dollar secures a box seat, or *palco,* where you may be free from intrusion and where you will bless your stars that you are not down amongst that fighting, swearing, altogether disreputable crowd below; for it is a rough and noisy collection of all sorts of Puerto Riqueños, and for Babel-like sounds and confusion generally not even the redoubtable stock exchange can equal it. You are sure to be surprised at several things, if this be your first visit to the *valla:* the amount of betting that goes on, despite the apparent confusion; the quiet manner in which all bets are settled, when you fully expected to see a score of contestants weltering in their gore; the smallness of the birds and the amount of pluck they possess to the square inch, and the skill, even science, requisite to become a first-class manipulator of fighting cocks.

A common sight in the streets of San Juan, early in the morning, is that of numerous gamecocks staked out by short strings to pegs driven into the sidewalks. There they seem to imagine themselves strictly in evidence, and keep up a crowing to inform their neighbours that they are as good as anybody else, if not a little better. If by chance one of the cocks gets loose there is soon a dead bird for somebody to pay for. The birds are as carefully groomed as any blooded horse, and a part of their keepers' duty is to keep them in fine fettle for fighting. To see their owners pass along, from one to another, and give each one a "morning refresher" is one of the sights of San Juan. First, taking one of the cocks up in his hands (after having filled his mouth with water), he lifts each wing successively and squirts a fine stream beneath, as a Chinese laundryman dampens his linen; then he does the same to the head and neck, and carefully deposits the cock on the pavement. Thus each one has his "pick-me-up-in-the-morning," which is considered as essential to his health as a cocoanut cocktail is to his owner's.

In the various market places of Puerto Rico you will see numberless fowl in wicker coops, the air always resounding with their challenges and counter-challenges of defiance. Even the negro on the corner who sells *dulces* and *refrescos* is likely to have a rooster tied by a string to his stool, and will bet his "bottom dollar" upon that bird's invincibil-

FOODS, DRINKS, DIVERSIONS, ETC.   181

ity and pedigree. The while he has nothing to do—which is pretty much all the time—he devotes to the "education" of his pet. The peripatetic vender of various articles—such, for instance, as the seller of bread (who goes about with a basketful on his head and another in one hand of queer-looking, twisted loaves and rolls)—probably has a gamecock in a corner, which he will produce the moment any one is willing to match him. All the while he is crying out, "*Pan, pan, no quiere pan?*"—"Bread, bread, don't you want any bread?"—he has one eye out for a prospective set-to between his bird and some other.

But to return to the cockpit. After the crowd has gathered, the first business transacted is the weighing of the birds. It is usually done by a dignified, spectacled old gentleman, white-haired or bald (at least old enough to know better), and with an air of benevolence, who takes each bird separately, and carefully slinging it in a bandana, hitches it to one arm of a balance scale and notes its fighting weight with great exactness. It will certainly remind the American observer of that popular piece of statuary, usually found in the parlour of every first-class boarding house, known as "Weighing the Baby." But in this instance the old grocer with the Benjamin Franklin cast of countenance, who peers through his glasses so mildly, is the umpire, and the rooster takes the place of the baby! Surely no infant ever received such attention from fond parent as this skinny bird, with its plucked neck and back, and tail deprived of its chief ornamental plumes. He is coddled and cuddled as though worth his weight in gold—as he is, for the average price of a bird of fair quality only is from fifteen to twenty dollars, and there are not many for sale at any price whatever.

The manner of play is always settled before the fight begins, as to whether it shall be *de cuchillo* —literally, with knives or gaffs, sharp and terrible —or *al pico*—without artificial spurs. These preliminaries arranged, each man takes his bird to the middle of the arena, and placing him in position lets him go, facing the enemy. There is no hesitation on the part of either combatant, and the feathers fly at once. The contestants are small, but game to the backbone, and are only separated when one or the other is completely exhausted. This seldom happens before one of them has an eye gouged out, or his neck and head laid bare and bleeding to the bone.

And all this takes place in the midst of a perfect pandemonium of howls and yells, which subside the moment each pair has fought it out, when the bets are paid punctiliously and in order. Each bird has his backer, like a pugilist in a prize fight; also there is an umpire, to whom appeals are frequently made. Exact and known rules regulate proceedings, and wounded birds are allowed to be succoured under certain conditions. Perhaps a cock may become temporarily blinded by dust or blood. He is then tenderly raised by his backer and a little rum or alum water squirted through a quill into his eyes.

No pair is removed until one of the twain is dead or dying, and even then, with the defeated cock gasping in his death agonies, the victor hangs to him to the last. The winner has hardly time to crow exultantly—which he is sure to do—when he is taken away to make room for another pair, equally eager, equally full of fight; one of them, perhaps both, destined to be laid prone and mangled on the sawdust.

No, there may be more noise, display, and bluster in the bullfight; there may be more gore, more risk to the human participant; but there is something lacking there which the cockfight supplies. It is found in the pitting together of two creatures to whom the fight is mutually interesting, while in the case of the bullfight the enjoyment is pretty much all on one side. As the old squire said of fox hunting: "The horses like it; the dogs like it; the men like it; and, egad, we don't know but that the fox likes it, too!"

There is some doubt about the bull's perfect enjoyment in being prodded by *picadores*, goaded by *capeadores*, tormented by *banderilleros*, etc., let alone the play of the *espada* until he doesn't know whether he is on his head or his heels; but there is no doubt whatever as to the zest with which two gamecocks spring at each other's throat and proceed at once to feather pulling and bloodletting.

The most approved pastime here, as in Spain, is the noble game of bull-fighting, but as the natives usually lack the means to encourage the importation of a good "line" of fighters, human and taurine, they have to console themselves with the fowls. Now and then an opera company is induced to make a venture here; the theatre always has its devotees, and local musical societies extend and swell the harmonies evoked by the ever-present military band, which frequently plays in the plazas.

It may be needless to add that, being of Spanish origin, the people of Puerto Rico are extremely fond of music. Here, as in Spain, may be seen numerous strolling bands of guitar and mandolin players, and at evening time the air is filled with music. Peculiar to the island, indeed, is a certain instrument which, though by courtesy called "musical," yet may not seem so to the unaccustomed ear. This is the "guira"—pronounced *huirra*—a native gourd, a foot or two feet long, with a triangular hole cut into the inner curve of its neck, and its back scarified with notches extending half way around and two thirds its length.

This gourd has its recognised place in every native "band," for in the hands of an expert, a rhythmic, swishing sound is produced by the rubbing of the scarified surface with a two-tined steel fork, or even an umbrella rib. The sound evoked accentuates and adds volume to the music, and when one has become accustomed to the noise (something like the soft shuffle of feet on a sanded floor), the effect is far from disagreeable.

Although the Americans, meaning the inhabitants of the United States, have a world-wide reputation for the concocting of insidious and palate-tickling beverages, we must turn to the tropics for the greatest variety of cooling "refreshers." While our summer is a season of short duration, and really hot weather is at best but intermittent, below the line of 23° 28′ north latitude, or within the tropics, "perpetual summer" is indeed no mere figure of speech.

The hotter the climate in which man dwells, of course the more he is prone to drink, and it follows, as a matter of course, that people who have dwelt a long time in a tropical region should have a greater variety and more attractive assortment of tipples than those who have only a taste of warm weather interlarded between long spaces of winter cold. Where, then, Old Sol reigns with undisputed sway, as in the West Indies, the perspiring people are "driven to drink," though not necessarily to drunkenness.

In the "great houses" of the old planters, now so lamentably few, the well-stocked sideboard is vastly more than a tradition. It is ever in evidence, and is the first article of furniture which greets the eyes of the thirsty traveller as he enters the hospitable mansion, tired and heated from a long ride in the sun.

The planter's wife, or his housekeeper, has already anticipated the stranger's desires and compounded a pitcher of drink ere he has landed at the door. Immediately after the introduction and before being taken away by his host to remove the dust from his garments, the newly-arrived is invited to wash the dust from his throat. If it be late in the afternoon and dinner be near at hand—as all good travellers fervently pray may be the case—into the pitcher is inserted a queer-looking stick about a foot and a half in length and with spreading prongs at the " business end." This is twirled about rapidly between the perpendicular palms of the host or hostess, until the contents of the jorum are stirred to a froth, and then the stick is withdrawn and the liquid poured out—to be sent " where it will do the most good."

The drink—well, it may be a gin or brandy cocktail, or the more insidious " shrub " or " cashew " punch, but whatever it is it will be worth the imbibing, as an experiment if nothing more. As for the stick, it is called a " swizzler," and may be bought in the market place of any of the more southern West Indian islands, such as Guadeloupe, St. Lucia, or Barbados. It is found in the fields and forests and brought in for sale by old women and children. It is slender and straight, with four or five prongs at one end, sticking out at right angles to the stem, and from its peculiar shape is used as an egg-beater and to intimately mix the ingredients of cocktails and the like. It creates, even in plain drinks, a peculiar froth, owing to the mucilaginous quality of the cambium layer, or inner bark, which is left on when the stick is peeled.

Thus does Nature provide for bibulous man in those regions where he is inclined to imbibe the most and where there is no "liquor law" to interfere with her generous provisions.

The Cubans and Puerto Ricans are remarkably abstemious, and those of Spanish birth, especially of the poorer class, eat little and drink less. But there is one thing in which they have well-nigh reached perfection, and that is the art of concocting "soft" drinks. If they may follow out their inclination and ancient custom, they begin the day with a cup of black coffee or chocolate, the latter so thick that it may be eaten with a fork, and perhaps accompanied by a small roll or thin biscuit. During the heat of the day the natives drink sparingly, but after the cool breezes of evening have set in the cafés are crowded with the seekers after *refrescos*, or cooling beverages. A *refresco* is literally a "refresher," generally in shape of a *limonada* (limeade) or *naranjada* (orangeade), while the favourite with the fair sex is the *orchata* (sweetened and diluted milk of almonds), and a drink made by dipping into water small rolls composed of the white of egg and sugar, and called *panales*.

The lower-orders content themselves with a mild tipple of barley water (*cebada*) or *la chicha*, which is water with toasted corn and sugar in it; *zambum-*

bia is diluted cane juice, as *aguardiente* (or fire water) is the same juice distilled, vulgarly known in English as rum. Another drink, a sort of sweet beer, is made from fermented pineapple rinds and is very delicious.

Better drink nothing stronger than chocolate before noon; or, still better, nothing stronger at all! In Cuba and Puerto Rico the people rarely indulge in anything stronger than the *vino Catalan;* at balls and parties, champagne. Though they drink early, some of them, and many of them often, it is chiefly of harmless beverages. In the French and English islands there are many who begin the day with a cocoanut and gin cocktail as an "eye opener," follow it with native rum at intervals, and end with ale or beer, brandy and champagne. The most healthful drink, the English West Indian will tell you, is rum, but not less than three years old. It has no "pernicious effects," he says, if sufficiently matured, and it is a tradition in the islands that rum will not improve with age even, unless it is kept in "the wood."

There is a wide range to the tropic tipples, the basis of most of them being the distilled juice of the sugar-cane, and there are delicious "punches" innumerable. One of the most nectareous of these concoctions is the "cashew punch," which is made by mixing the fragrant juice of the *acajou* with sugar (*quantum suf.*), rum (*quantum libet*), and served with a grating of aromatic nutmeg floating atop. It is a drink too good for the gods, the West Indians say, but just the thing for bibulous man. In the olden time, when every planter distilled his own rum, a certain delightful liquor called " shrub " was in vogue, the basis of which was rum, with one fourth its weight of sugar added to it, and one sixteenth lime juice. But both "shrub" and planter, so racy of the West Indian soil, will be difficult to find, alas! at the present time, in Cuba and Puerto Rico.

Water, the natives say, numbers more victims than rum, and while that of the mountain streams may be pure and potable, one should use with caution the *agua* of the towns and cities. Even if it has been filtered through the great porous drip-stones, which every house possesses, it is not always safe to drink. The fevers and various intestinal diseases from which our soldiers suffered, were mainly caused by drinking impure water.

Perhaps the strangest sight of the Puerto Rican market is the beast of burden, either horse or donkey, but always small and half starved, entirely covered by a heap of grass or fodder. The native horse has been taught to turn up his nose at anything in the shape of oats or grain of any kind, his regular rations consisting of green grass and fodder from a peculiar species of corn, which is raised exclusively for its tops, which are sweet and succulent, and known as *maloja*. The *malojero*, as the small farmer furnishing the fodder is called, comes from a long distance out in the country, riding atop his beastie's burden, and looking something like a monkey on an ambulatory corn stack. These *malojeros* are the most numerous attendants at the market places, for every owner of a horse or jackass in town or city must have his matutinal *maloja*, and is actually dependent upon the arrival of the countryman for it.

Next in point of numbers are the milkmen, who likewise ride on top their loads, or, rather, astride, between their cans, coming in at a jerky trot, which, with the terrible heat of the morning hour, serves to stir the *leche* into butyric consistency. The *lechero* never dismounts, but rides up in front of a customer's house and shouts "*Leche!*" in a voice fit to wake the dead, smoking his cigarette the while he ladles out the liquid from between his legs, his feet level with the horse's ears. Sometimes the cow is driven to your door, and milked on the spot.

After the milkman comes the baker, who dispenses the product of his ovens from the back of horse or burro, and is not seemingly happy unless he has sat all the morning on the bag of bread which he brings along for sale.

But the *panadero* is a sweet and savory spectacle compared with the butcher, the *carnicero*, who drags reeking carcasses into town, wobbling gruesomely in a cart, or more frequently hanging from hooks in frames on horseback. All the *mataderos*, or slaughterhouses, are outside the city limits, with troops of wild dogs and turkey buzzards (the local scavengers) fighting and snarling over entrails and garbage.

Then there is the chicken vender, who brings his cargo of fowl to market in great wicker coops slung across the back of his beast, he himself sitting, as usual, astride between. There is no society for the prevention of cruelty to animals in any Spanish country, and every man may do what seems to him best with anything he owns.

Housekeeping in the West Indies is not without its drawbacks, as may be inferred from the mention already made of insects, such as ants and flies, which invade every house, at some time or other, the constant heat, lack of ice and cool water, and of many modern conveniences. In the country districts ice is never thought of as an adjunct to the household "outfit," or even as a luxury. The style of cooking is that of old Spain, over a small pot or brazier of charcoal, while roasts, steaks, and chops are less in vogue than stews or ragouts. And it is a strange inconsistency that moves the otherwise neat and careful householder to have the kitchen, cistern, and cesspool nearly always contiguous! One should never invade the Spanish kitchen unless proof against all squeamishness regarding the preparation of food. There are exceptions, but they are rare, in which the kitchens and sculleries are scrupulously clean.

The writer has partaken of foods cooked in Spain, in Mexico, in Cuba, South America, and Puerto Rico, and can not aver that there is any appreciable difference in their preparation. To ascertain, then, the probable *menu* that will be placed before you at the hotel or boarding-house, it is only necessary to acquaint yourself with the Spanish style of cooking, which is a modified French, with many courses, savoury soups, light wines, numerous condiments, and fruits.

The business man goes to work in the morning with merely a cup of coffee, or coffee and a biscuit, to stay him until the first real meal of the day, which is the *almuerzo*, or breakfast, and usually served from eleven to twelve. This is a substantial repast, of five or six courses, ending with coffee and cigarettes, perhaps with a dash of rum, before or after the coffee. Dinner—*comida*—is eaten at six or seven o'clock, differing from breakfast only in being somewhat more substantial and prolonged, during which French clarets and Spanish wines are concomitants, and terminating with the inevitable black coffee and cigars or cigarettes. A commendable custom prevails in Cuba and Puerto Rico, among the business men, of taking the morning meal with their clerks, at a long table spread in a veranda or corridor of their establishment.

Between meals, or from about noon to three or four o'clock in the afternoon, all Puerto Rico indulges in the recuperative *siesta*, during which time it is as easy to drive a flourishing business in a cemetery as to attempt it in the commercial portion of a town or city. All tropical dwellers are early risers; the principal business of the day is transacted in the morning, the afternoon being devoted mainly to social calls, the clubs, casinos, promenades, and the evening also to recreation. Thus they have established a certain system in their daily duties, which doubtless, by its absence of friction, by insuring them against haste and worry, tends to the preservation of health and prolongation of life.

Cacao tree and fruit.

In this survey of the West Indian household we should not overlook an important member, or rather adjunct, of it, the washerwoman. She is just as black as she is painted, and that is usually very black indeed. Her hand is against every man, and every man's hand ought to be against her, for she maltreats man's belongings—his shirts and his cuffs and collars—in a manner that is fearful to behold. She lives on the outskirts of civilization, and has no recognised status in society. No one knows whence she comes; but there she is, waiting for the steamer to land, and with an overgrown lad or stout boatman to assist her to seize and carry away your soiled linen and cast-off clothing. If any article is particularly nice or valuable, she appropriates that as her perquisite, or else so desperately mauls it that it returns to you having no semblance to anything you ever saw before, least of all to anything you ever possessed.

She has no washtub, no scrubbing board, and sometimes no soap, some native roots or berries serving in lieu of the last. But she carries the policeman's weapon—a club—and wields it in a way that would put one of the "finest" to the blush.

It is early morning when, having secured a pile of linen intrusted to her care by some guileless and inoffensive man, she slowly wends her way to the nearest river, or to the sea, with the bundle on her head. If, perchance, she carries a tub, it is one she has borrowed, and is taken along not for use, but merely as a "guarantee of good faith." She deposits her burden on the bank of the stream or shore of the sea, and then fills and lights her pipe. Others of her kind and persuasion come along, who fill their pipes and then sit down for a social confab. The ways and means of defeating the ends and aims of civilization are the chief topics of conversation, and when these are exhausted the real object of their mission—to destroy as many as possible of the garments intrusted to their care—is commenced. The washerwoman is gregarious, and she flocks as much as possible with her own sex and profession.

Each one has near her a broad, smooth stone, upon which she spreads out a portion of the day's catch, and then proceeds to reduce it to a pulpy, indistinguishable mass. She souses it in the stream, slams it against the rocks, then, having soaped it well, she falls to with her club. Not a button escapes, not a hole in any one unfortunate garment that is not made larger and wider! The sound of blows, delivered with fatal effect, proclaims the scene of conflict, and may be heard from afar. No mere mortal man has ever been known to witness the fray and return to tell the tale without emotion. After the clothes are sufficiently soused and mutilated they are wrung dry, spread out on the stones or on a thorny cactus, and left to bleach in the sun. The rougher the stones or the thornier the cactus bush the better, in the estimation of the laundress.

Then she takes home her handiwork, throws it into a corner, where the pickaninnies sleep on it a few nights, and finally has the hardihood to present a claim to the owner of the linen for damages. Lafcadio Hearn, who has written sympathetic sketches of the creoles, draws a pathetic picture of the trials and tribulations of the washerwoman. She is exposed, he says, to the heat of the tropical sun by day, standing knee deep in the water of chill mountain streams; she is often the victim of torrential rains and hurricanes; her skin is baked to a turn, and the clothes she guards washed away by the rising flood.

XIV.

THE INDIANS OF PUERTO RICO.

THERE are no Indians now in Puerto Rico, though at one time, before the coming of the Spaniards, it has been estimated they existed here to the number of more than a million. Just why the *conquistadores* should have set out to exterminate the original inhabitants of the island, it is difficult to say, but probably from an inherent " cussedness." They were pious, these early discoverers of America, and they wanted all the Indians they came in contact with to be pious also; and as the latter could not understand the mysteries of the newcomers' religion, they paid the penalty in extermination. To adapt that much-quoted and misleading couplet anent the landing of the Pilgrim Fathers:

> The *conquistadores* fell on their knees;
> Then they fell on the aborigines!

Commencing at the very beginnings of Puerto Rican history, going back to that eventful year, 1493, in which the island was discovered: we have it, on the authority of the Spaniards themselves, that the aboriginal peoples of the West Indies were all very cleanly and attentive to the care of their persons. And that they bathed early and bathed often may have been the real cause of Spanish dislike, for if there is any antipathy that is racial, it is said to be that of the Dons against the general use of water in ablution! Says a Spanish historian, writing of the Moors and the conquest of Granada: "Water seems more necessary to these infidels than bread, for they make use of it in repeated daily ablutions, enjoined by their damnable religion, and employ it in baths, and in a thousand other idle and extravagant modes, of which we Spaniards and Christians make but little account!"

It has been stated that the Spaniard looked upon an "altogether" bath, or "tub," as a sort of extreme unction, to be taken, if at all, but once in a lifetime. This may be a slander; but does not history inform us of a certain Spanish queen who vowed not to change her linen until a city her forces were then besieging should be taken, and who kept her vow, though the siege lasted a year?

But, be this as it may, the natives of Puerto Rico went about nearly naked, yet unashamed, and virtuous—until the coming of the Spaniards. And, as they bathed frequently and were, exteriorly at least, cleanly and wholesome, the Spaniards looked upon this as a reproach. They might, the Spaniards reasoned, have clean and shining countenances, but they gave no thought to their souls' salvation; hence they were, in all probability, inwardly corrupt and unclean, therefore fit subjects for extermination; and exterminated they were, accordingly.

The natives of all the Greater Antilles were considered as of the same stock, and probably descended from the Arrowacks of Guiana, in South America, " a race of Indians to whose noble qualities the most honourable testimony is borne; and here all inquiry concerning the origin of our islanders seems to terminate." At the time of the Spanish discovery, the historian Las Casas computed them at more than six million; but this, probably, is an exaggerated estimate. Those of Hispaniola, or Santo Domingo, Oviedo estimated at one million and Peter Martyr at one million two hundred thousand. They were, indeed, so numerous, says Las Casas, that the islands swarmed with Indians as an ant-hill with ants! Bryan Edwards, the historian of Jamaica, compares them with the Otaheites, " with whom they seem to have many qualities in common." They cultivated large areas in maize and manioc, made immense canoes from the cedar and ceiba trees, which they gunwaled and pitched with bitumen or natural asphaltum. They wore a cotton girdle around the waist, while the cannibal Caribs of the more southern islands went entirely naked. They were of good shape and stature, but less robust and valiant than the Caribs, and their colour darker, being a deep, clear brown. All the islanders compressed the heads of infants artificially, but in a different manner: " The Caribs elevated the forehead, making the head look like two sides of a square; but the natives of the larger islands compressed the occiput, rendering the crown of the head so thick that a Spanish broadsword would sometimes break upon it." The practice of the Spanish settlers of making this a test of skill at sword-play—as to which of them could most skilfully crack open an Indian's skull, or neatly decapitate him—is a speaking commentary on the brutality of those first Spaniards in these islands. In addition to this playful manner of disposing of the redskins, they sometimes burned them alive, and roasted them over slow fires, as witnessed against them by their own ecclesiastical teacher, Las Casas.

These things are mentioned merely as showing some of the causes of extermination; although the ultimate and perhaps chief cause was the excessive labour in the mines, initiated by Columbus himself. And yet, says Martyr, " theirs was an honest countenance, coarse, but not gloomy, for it was enlivened by confidence and softened by compassion." We know that they had native songs and hymns, called *arietos;* an idea of a Deity, and a multitude of minor gods; that they made articles of pottery, common vessels, as well as some with unique adornments, hammocks, huts, and chairs of wood and stone. When Bartholomew Columbus visited the Indian queen, Anacoana, he was presented with fourteen chairs of ebony, and sixty earthen vessels " ornamented with fantastic figures of living animals."

They obtained and wrought the native gold from mountain streams, and it was the Spaniards' lust for gold that rang their death-knell, for all the Indians were divided into *encomiendas* and *repartimientos,* for labour in the field and mines. Without entering into further details: in fifteen years the Spaniards reduced the Indians of Santo Domingo from more than a million to less than sixty thousand; and in 1585 Sir Francis Drake reported not an Indian alive.

Said a celebrated French professor to a resident of this island only a few years ago: " The most acceptable present you can make our museum is a skull of one of the aborigines of your island, for there is not one in all Europe to-day!"

However true this statement may be, it is certain that crania from Santo Domingo and Puerto Rico are desiderata in our own museums, though the writer has found them at different times. All the remarks anent these Indians will apply to the aborigines of Puerto Rico, who were of the same stock and ultimately shared their fate. Though lying near to the island of Santo Domingo, and separated from it by a narrow channel, Puerto Rico was not discovered by Columbus until his second voyage, and not settled before 1508 or 1509. Ponce de Leon, who afterward became famous through his search for the Fountain of Youth, landed there and overran the island with his soldiers, finding a people similar to the Dominicans, cultivators of the soil and following the pursuits of peace.

It was not many years before these innocent Indians had gone the way of the others, and the populous country was devastated. The last of them perished long ago, so long that not even tradition can inform us accurately as to the uses of the hundreds of articles they once manufactured and left behind them. But, of all the West Indian aborigines, they were the farthest advanced in the crude arts of primitive humanity. Their pottery is highly ornamental, their stone implements, of warfare and husbandry, are unique; "their implements of industry, so far as we have recovered them, are the most beautiful in the world; their artists were prodigies in design and workmanship."

One of the most complete collections in the world, illustrating the arts and economy of ancient Americans, is the assemblage of Puerto Rican antiquities in the Smithsonian Institution at Washington, a gift of the late George Latimer, of San Juan. Mr. Latimer was a resident merchant, who for many years collected all the aboriginal antiquities he could find, and finally sent them to Washington, a priceless gift to his country's capital. This collection was long ago the subject of a monograph by the talented Prof. O. T. Mason, who published, in 1877, this most valuable contribution to ethnographical literature, fully illustrated.

Although the common "celts" and ordinary stone implements are found elsewhere, yet there are several types found nowhere else in the world. These are the so-called "mammiform stones" and "collars." The mammiform stones are most suggestive of a human form buried under a mountain, with head and feet protruding. The name was suggested by the conical or conoid prominence in

The sea grape.

the centre, and of course is wholly arbitrary; but to any one who has seen the rounded and pyramidal hills of Puerto Rico, the resemblance is very evident.

They are as truly *sui generis* as the "collars," which likewise are peculiar to this island, absolutely unique, and receive their appellation from their resemblance to horse collars, though of stone. Some of these syenite collars weigh as much as sixty-five pounds each, and are from nineteen to twenty-three inches in length and from fifteen to seventeen in breadth. Many specimens are shown in the Smithsonian collection, in various stages of elaboration, but the majority are beautifully finished and polished, with bosses and panels, sometimes on one side and sometimes on the other. This peculiarity of ornamentation has given rise to the distinction of "right- and left-shouldered" collars, presuming that they may have served some use in pairs.

Just what that use was no one can tell, the historians being silent on the subject, while the early Spaniards were too busy prodding the live Indians, to concern themselves about the dead ones and their arts. But an old priest once told the writer, when in Puerto Rico, that the Indians made these collars for the purpose of having them buried with them in their graves. They were the peculiar property of the caciques, and each workman spent nearly a lifetime in laboriously carving out a huge collar of stone, that when he died it might be placed over his head, on his breast, thus securely fastening him down in his last resting-place, and defying the efforts of the devil to carry him away!

In this explanation, however, one may detect the ecclesiastical intrusion; for no theologer, no matter of what belief, is entirely happy unless he can fasten upon an aboriginal people a firm belief in a devil, or some evil genius of the supernatural world. However, this explanation is as good as any, since no one, not even the ethnologist, has offered a better. The same may be said of the strange objects called "masks" or human faces carved of solid stone, and which, Professor Mason thinks, may have been used as club-heads or banner stones.

The aborigines of this island possessed the same animal and plant resources as those of Santo Domingo, the flora and fauna being similar, and their dwellings were formed from the same materials. In neither island are there remains of stately structures, or any indications of buildings which were made of less perishable material than palm leaves or native woods. In both islands, also, the aboriginal name—*bohio*—is still applied to the rude

THE INDIANS OF PUERTO RICO. 207

hut of palm wood thatched with leaves and grass, as distinguished from the more pretentious *casa* of the Spaniard and city dweller. It truth, many, if not most, of the names applied in Puerto Rico to towns, districts, woods, and plants, are directly derived from the aboriginal appellations.

Nevertheless, as already shown, not a single direct descendant of the millions, or many thousands, found at the time of discovery, remains in any island of the Greater Antilles. All have perished, root and branch, and have left behind only these mute memorials of their former existence here. All we have to instruct us, else, is the scant information to be gleaned from the pages of old historians, who at best could not appreciate the value of ethnological material, considered strictly as such. Only in a casual manner, and merely as incidental to the historical narrative, are we informed of the most valuable " finds " (of Columbus, for instance) in America. The nation that destroyed the libraries of the Moors in Spain, and the picture-writings of the Aztecs in Mexico, has never shown any inclination to preserve the memorials of Indians whom its soldiers and settlers combined to exterminate.

XV.

A CHAPTER OF HISTORY.

Now that Puerto Rico has become a colonial dependency of the United States, there will never be any likelihood of future Spanish ownership of American islands, nor of Spanish fleets again cruising in Hispano-American waters. It has taken four hundred years to deliver the two Americas from the misrule of Spain; but at last that deliverance has come, and the historic flag of Hispania will no longer float over forts and castles where for centuries it has been a familiar object, feared, hated, and revered.

But, with the passing of Spanish authority, the best of Spain yet remains behind, for no other country of Europe could have furnished us with such a stock of romantic traditions and poetic associations as this land of Goth and Saracen. Her *conquistadores* came here fresh from the conquest of the Moors, and they brought with them not alone tales and traditions, but swords and arquebuses from the battlefields of Andalusia. The writer has found, in Santo Domingo and Puerto Rico, and had the pleasure of bringing to the United States, veritable " Toledo blades," that had been fashioned on the banks, and tempered with the waters, of the golden Tagus.

Thus we find the beginnings of Puerto Rican history invested with the glamour of Old World association, for the great navigator, Columbus, discovered the island in 1493, and the great *conquistador*, Ponce de Leon, first visited it in 1508. Finding it inhabited by a docile and intelligent people, and receiving from the native cacique, Agueynaba, rich specimens of gold obtained from the river-beds, De Leon returned to Santo Domingo, only to revisit Puerto Rico the next year with soldiers and settlers for colonization.

The first settlement was called Caparra, to-day known as the Pueblo Viejo, and not far distant from the present capital, San Juan, for the site of which it was later abandoned. Caparra was founded in 1510, and the same year the Indians, though the most tractable of subjects under ordinary rule, rebelled against the atrocities committed by the Spaniards. They had given freely of their gold and provisions, had allowed the strangers to roam the island at will and choose sites for their towns; but when it became evident that these white men, who had come up out of the sea, were determined to reduce them to slavery, they revolted.

The Spaniards had told them, and at first they had believed, that the newcomers were immortal, sent from heaven for their edification; but soon the most observant of the Indians, and notably Cacique Agueynaba, had their doubts. At all events, they concluded that if the Spanish heaven was to be the abode of the Spanish settlers and soldiers, they would have none of it. Agueynaba resolved to test the alleged immortality of the Spaniards, and so, acting under his orders, one day two Indians captured a Spanish soldier, and held his head under water for two hours. Then they dragged him to the bank of the stream and sat by his side during two days, by which time it was so evident, even to the dull comprehension of a savage, that he was dead, that they reported the fact to their cacique. The very stream is known, and is pointed out to-day, where this interesting experiment, which led to such dire consequences for the Spaniards, was carried out.

The Indians were brave enough, but they were always peacefully inclined; and, again, they were equipped only with bows and arrows, wooden spears and stone battle-axes, as against the Span-

A CHAPTER OF HISTORY. 211

iards with their keen swords and terrible weapons spitting fire and smoke. In the insurrection that followed, though all the Spaniards found outside the town of Caparra were put to death, yet the Indians were beaten and later driven to the mines, where the unaccustomed labours soon accomplished their extermination.

That same year, or the year after, in 1512, the settlers took measures for the introduction of negro slaves from Africa to fill the places of the Indians killed in the mines and in the fields.

In the year 1512, having put the settlement in good order, Governor Ponce de Leon sailed on that voyage through the Bahamas resulting in the discovery of Florida, which has immortalized his name. In the year 1521, after having great difficulties with the cannibal Caribs of the southern islands, and, in fact, having suffered defeat at their hands, De Leon again sailed northwardly, in quest of the fabled Fountain of Youth, which he had sought and failed to discover on his previous voyage. He found a soldier's grave only, for he was wounded by a poisoned arrow on the coast of Florida, taken to Havana, and died before he could reach Puerto Rico. His remains were carried thither, and in the city of San Juan they are preserved to-day, where also may be seen the house he built—the

Casa Blanca—and a monument erected to his memory.

The first settlers were terribly afflicted during their stay at Caparra, for a visitation of ants, which drove them all from their houses, was soon followed by an epidemic of small-pox, and this by that dread disease, resulting from their excesses with the Indians, the origin of which has been ascribed to the West Indian islands. In 1529 the town of San Germán was sacked and burned by French privateers, who committed great cruelties on the coast peoples, and the next year many settlers were carried off to be eaten by the Caribs. A romantic outcome of this invasion was the expedition for the recovery of the captives, led by the wife of an influential citizen, only to find that the chief prisoner had been killed and probably devoured.

It was not until 1516 or 1517 that English vessels first came into the Caribbean, being two ships of war under Sebastian Cabot and Sir Thomas Pert. Two years after that the first English trading vessel arrived at Puerto Rico. Captain John Hawkins followed in 1565, and Captain Francis Drake in 1572, but no settlement was founded by either. It was during this audacious voyage of Drake's that the gallant seaman climbed a tree on the highest point of Darien, and saw for the first time the Pacific Ocean, which he later sailed across, being knighted by Elizabeth on his return, in 1581. He was then engaged in the exciting sport of "singeing the King of Spain's whiskers"—in other words, of attacking his ships in home ports and harrying the harbours of his foreign possessions. It was his shrewd policy, in attacking and destroying so many of the Spanish storeships in the harbour of Cadiz, that delayed the "invincible Armada," which was fitted out by Philip II to invade England, and aided in accomplishing its ultimate destruction.

As the Spanish settlements of South America increased, and from the interior country as well as across the isthmus, from the mines of Peru, came vast treasures of gold and silver, which were taken to Spain in slow-sailing galleons, Sir Francis and his companion freebooters had most royal sport and royal plunder. As early as 1563, or the year before Shakespeare was born, Hawkins made a profitable voyage to Guinea and back, bringing to the West Indies a cargo of slaves. He was the original slaver, as his friend and kinsman, Drake, was the original royal freebooter. In the interim of his slaving voyages he sacked and bombarded Spanish cities in the Caribbean, or bombarded them first and sacked them afterward, and Drake did the same.

This pair of precious privateers made the Caribbean Sea an exceedingly warm place for the Spanish galleons, and for the Spanish settlements as well.

The Spanish ships and settlements afforded glorious sport for Drake, Hawkins, Raleigh, and all that rollicking crew of adventurers, for many years, until they wearied the King of Spain to the extent that he fitted out the great armada. Then, indeed, these old sea lions had Philip " on the hip," for they worried and harried those big sea castles and bulky galleons until, of the sixscore and more which sailed so gallantly out of the port of Cadiz, in the summer of 1588, intent upon the wiping of England from the map of nations—what with the assistance of the elements—not threescore ever gained Spanish port again. And with the Spanish ships, so with the Spanish islands: one by one they fell into the hands of the British lion, until, of all those which once dotted the western seas, not one remained save Cuba and Puerto Rico; and these have now fallen to a scion of the lion, who inherits all his thrift, and, 'tis said, also his courage at sea and on land!

In 1586 Drake was commissioned by Queen Elizabeth to do all the harm he could to Spanish shipping, and he again chose the Caribbean Sea as the theatre of his exploits. It would have sorely wounded the dignity of either Sir Francis, or his kinsman Sir John Hawkins, had they been classed with the pirates of that day and later, but so the Spaniards viewed them, and so their contemporaries called them. The last voyage of both these worthies was made in company, and both were dead before it terminated. Both were buried at sea, Hawkins off the eastern end of Puerto Rico and Drake off a port of the Spanish Main.

The fitting out and equipment of this expedition were not surpassed by that of 1585. Its destination in the first place was intended for Puerto Rico, where the Queen (Elizabeth) had received information that a vast treasure had been brought, intended to be sent thence for the use of the King of Spain in completing the third grand armament (the second, the Armada, having been destroyed by Drake) which he had in contemplation for the invasion of England.

The expedition left Plymouth August 28, 1595. . . . On the 30th of September the Francis, being of Sir John Hawkins's division, a bark of thirty-five tons, was chased by five of the king's frigates, or *zabras*—being ships of two hundred tons—which came for the treasure at San Juan de Puerto Rico. The Francis, mistaking them for companions, was taken in sight of our caravels. The Spaniards, indifferent to human suffering, left her driving in the sea, with three or four hurt or sick men, and took the rest of her people into their ships and returned to San Juan.

The squadron intended to pass through the Virgin Islands, but here, says Hakluyt, "Sir John Hawkins was extreme sick, which his sickness began upon neues of the taking of the Francis." Remaining here two days, they tarried two days more in a sound (Sir Francis Drake's Channel) which Drake in his barge had discovered. They then stood for the eastern end of Puerto Rico, where Sir John Hawkins breathed his last.

Sir Thomas Baskerville now took possession of the Garland, as second in command. The fleet came to anchor at a distance of two miles or less from the eastern side of the town of San Juan, where, says Hakluyt, " we received from their forts and places where they planted ordnance, some twenty-eight great shot, the last of which stroke the Admiral's ship, through the misen, and the last but one stroke her through the quarter into the steerage; the General being there at supper, and stroke the stool from under him, but hurt him not; but hurt at the same table Sir Nicholas Clifford, Mr. Browne, Capt. Stratford, with one or two more. Sir Nicholas Clifford and Master Browne died of these hurts."

Drake was certainly imprudent in suffering his squadron to take up anchorage so near to the means of annoyance, but his former visit had no doubt taught the enemy the prudence of being better prepared for any future occasion, and it is somewhat remarkable that Drake should not have observed his usual caution. Browne was an old and particular favourite of his.

The following morning the whole fleet came to anchor before the point of the town without the harbour, where they remained till nightfall, and then twenty-five pinnaces, boats, and shallops, well-manned and furnished with fireworks and small shot, entered the roadstead. . . . The great castle, or galleon, the object of the present enterprise, had been completely repaired and was on the point of sailing when certain intelligence of the intended attack by Drake reached the island. Then the whole of the treasure was landed—said to amount to four million dollars—the galleon was sunk at the mouth of the harbour, a floating barrier of masts and spars was laid on each side of her, near to the forts and castles, so as to render the entrance impassable; within this breakwater were moored five *zabras*, all the women and infirm people moved to the interior, and those only left in town who were capable to aid in its defence.

A heavy fire was opened on the English ships, but the adventurers persisted in their attempt until they had lost, by their own account, some forty or fifty men killed and as many wounded; but there was consolation in the thought that, by burning, drowning, and killing, the loss of the Spaniards could not be less—in fact, a great deal more, for the five *zabras* and a large ship of four hundred tons were burnt, and their several cargoes of silk, oil, and wine destroyed.

218   PUERTO RICO AND ITS RESOURCES.

Defeated in their main object, but not disheartened, the advance party of pinnaces and small vessels returned to the fleet in the offing, and remained at anchor the next day, then removed to the southwest point of the island, to wash the ships and refresh the crews.

Drake did not return to San Juan, but contented himself with levying tribute or burning towns on the Caribbean side of the island. His fleet then sailed for Nombre de Dios, and on the 28th of January, 1596, while the fleet was off Porto Bello, Drake breathed his last, and was buried at sea in a leaden coffin. He was succeeded in command by Sir Thomas Baskerville, who, while returning to England, fell in with a Spanish fleet off the Isle of Pines, and gave it battle. The English had the best of it, but the Spanish admiral (after the Spanish fashion) subsequently issued a bulletin, claiming a glorious victory. Baskerville was so incensed that on his return home he posted the Spanish admiral as a liar and challenged him to a duel, but nothing ever came of it.

In 1698 another English squadron, of twenty-two ships, attacked San Juan, but was almost entirely destroyed by the elements, a furious hurricane sinking many vessels and delivering their crews into the hands of their enemies. In 1702 a

A calabash tree.

Dutch squadron, and also an English, were driven off from San Juan, but a Puerto Rican fleet, fitted out to attack the British, was totally destroyed by a hurricane; so that the islanders were now convinced that the previous and similar disaster to the foreigners was not altogether a visitation of Providence, as they had at first regarded it.

The seventeenth century was one of trouble and disaster to the Spaniards in the West Indies, particularly in Puerto Rico, for the French and English buccaneers were then flourishing. Divided into two bands, these pirates committed terrible depredations under the name of *bucaneros* and *filibusteros*, their headquarters being first in the island of St. Kitts, whence they were dislodged by Don Federico Toledo, who dropped upon them with an expedition from San Juan de Puerto Rico in 1629–'30, and finally in the island of Tortuga, off the coast of Haiti.

The eighteenth century was peaceful, in the main, but toward its close, or in 1797, after the Franco-Spanish alliance against England, the British made immediate preparations for weakening Spain through repeated attacks upon her colonies. A squadron was assembled in the West Indies under the command of Sir Ralph Abercromby, which attacked the Spanish fleet in the bay of Port of

Spain, island of Trinidad, with the result that the latter surrendered without firing a shot, and that noble island, together with two hundred pieces of artillery and an ambulance of ammunition and provisions, fell into British hands. As on the occasion of another Spanish surrender—that of Santiago de Cuba, to the Americans, in 1898—a condition agreed to was that all Spanish sailors and soldiers should be returned to Spain as soon as transports could be secured for the purpose. Thus History repeats itself; only in the former case there were but twenty-two hundred Spaniards to be repatriated, while in the modern instance there were nearly thirty thousand.

After the capture of Trinidad, which was confirmed in British possession in 1802, the English turned their eyes toward Puerto Rico, as being the nearest Spanish island of importance, and which, says the English historian of that day, writing in 1798, "under an enlightened government might be raised to an eminent rank in the colonial scale"!

Abercromby landed his troops off the little hamlet of Cangrejos, and made several determined attempts to take San Juan; but after two weeks of desultory bombarding and skirmishing was finally forced to depart, with a total loss of two hundred and thirty killed, wounded, and missing.

This was the last bombardment of San Juan until the premature attack upon its fortifications on May 12, 1898, by Admiral Sampson, of the United States navy. Although these old walls, mounted mainly with obsolete cannon and mortars, have been objects of ridicule for many years, yet it would seem that they are more nearly impregnable than modern earthworks; and it is not improbable that the world may some day witness a return to the picturesque fortifications of the great Vauban!

During the attack by Abercromby there were several desperate hand-to-hand encounters in the very streets of the city, which were barricaded and ditched. The Spanish loss, according to their own accounts, was forty-two killed and one hundred and fifty wounded; but they took prisoners, they claimed, more than the entire number which the British acknowledged as killed, wounded, and missing.

The present century has witnessed few serious disturbances in Puerto Rico, save those caused by sympathetic action with Spanish politics. Thus, during the second decade of the century, while Mexico and the Spanish-American colonies were engaged in throwing off their allegiance to the mother country, disturbances also occurred in

Puerto Rico, but not to an extent which seriously threatened the Spanish domination. Again, in the '30s, when Spain was agitated over the Spanish succession, Carlists and Separatists succeeded in making much trouble in the colony; but, in the main, with the exception of an uprising about thirty years ago, Puerto Rico has justified its title of " ever loyal and faithful isle."

In fact, the very features of the island lend themselves to the preservation of peace, for, while the island of Cuba affords secure hiding-places for innumerable insurgents, whence they may keep up a desultory but destructive warfare for months and years with impunity; in Puerto Rico, on the contrary, there are few points of vantage for the revolutionist. The cry of *" Viva Puerto Rico libre "* is as dear to the heart of the average Puerto-Riqueño as *" Viva Cuba libre "* is to the Cuban insurgent; but he has hardly had an opportunity for raising a banner with the patriotic sentiment inscribed thereon, before the Spanish soldiery have been upon him.

XVI.

AN AMERICAN POSSESSION.

No year, decade, or century has been so pregnant with important events to Puerto Rico since its discovery and conquest as the year 1898. For, in the summer of that year, consequent upon events with which we are all familiar, occurred the transfer of supreme authority over its governmental destinies from Spain to the United States. Immediately after the virtual declaration of war, involved in President McKinley's ultimatum to Spain, April 20, 1898, attention was directed to Puerto Rico, not only as a strategic base of operations, but as a possession prospectively valuable in itself.

The impression that it was foredoomed to capture by our fleets and armies was heightened when, the last week in April, the Spanish fleet, commanded by Admiral Cervera, consisting of four cruisers and battleships, and three torpedo boats and "destroyers," left the Cape de Verde Islands for West Indian waters. During nearly three weeks, when all America was in a feverish state of suspense as to the whereabouts of this formidable fleet, it was unknown whether its destination was to be some port of Cuba or of Puerto Rico. In the expectation that it would at least put in at San Juan to coal and refit, the United States fleet, under Admiral Sampson, cruised for a time in that vicinity, the ultimate result of this visit being the bombardment of the ancient fortifications of Puerto Rico's capital city. This bombardment, which took place May 12th, was a worse than useless expenditure of ammunition, as no adequate results were obtained, hardly an impression being made upon the age-worn battlements.

However, this, if nothing else, attracted universal attention to the island, and after the triumphant success of our arms at Santiago de Cuba, when his presence was no longer needed there, General Nelson A. Miles, with between three and four thousand troops, embarked for Puerto Rico. On the 25th of July, while all eyes were turned toward the northeast end of the island as his conjectural place of debarkation, General Miles suddenly appeared in the land-locked port of Guanica, on the southeast coast, and quickly captured it after a few shots ashore from the little gunboat Gloucester. A landing of troops was effected on the 26th, when, after a slight skirmish with the enemy, a march was made to Yauco, farther back in the hills; and on the 28th to Ponce, the largest city on this coast, which capitulated without firing a gun. Everywhere, indeed, the American troops were received with acclamation by the native residents of the island, who vied with each other in their attentions by the way, when they came out of their huts and houses with offerings of fruits, drinks, flowers, and shouted themselves hoarse with " *Viva los Americanos!* "

The Puerto Rican campaign had hardly begun when it was summarily ended—to the great chagrin of the commander-in-chief and all his subordinates—by the promulgation of the protocol between the United States and Spain, preliminary to the final treaty of peace. Although the casualties were slight, but few of our soldiers being killed in battle, yet at several points there was spirited fighting, and through it all our " boys " carried themselves with conspicuous gallantry. There were volunteer regiments from Massachusetts, Illinois, Wisconsin, Pennsylvania, and New York, besides infantry, batteries of artillery, and troops of cavalry from the regular service; and all did credit to the country that sent them out to fight its battles.

No time was lost in developing the strategy of

the commanding general, and when the unwelcome "protocol" was cabled to the island it found a military net spread for the enemy which would soon have resulted in his entire discomfiture. General Miles returned to the United States about the first week in September, and perhaps no better summary of his brief campaign can be given than in his own words, uttered soon after he landed on American soil:

As soon as a suitable escort could be obtained from the navy I left the coast of Cuba with thirty-four hundred men to seize and occupy the island of Puerto Rico. The place of landing had been so thoroughly advertised in communications sent over the French cable and in the newspapers of my own country, and telegraphed to Madrid and from there to San Juan, that, not having received the necessary appliances with which to disembark, I decided, after leaving the Windward Passage, to change my course and land on the south side of Puerto Rico, where the Spaniards were the least prepared and the least expecting to receive me, and where I knew that the disembarkation of the troops and the supplies could be most easily effected.

From the time of that disembarkation, during the following nineteen days of campaign, I kept the Spaniards guessing what the next move would be.

When they withdrew along the line of the

great military road between Ponce and San Juan they destroyed the bridges, obstructed the roads, and fortified strong positions in the mountain passes, and then were surprised to find that one column of my army was sweeping around the west of the island, capturing the principal cities and towns, while another had passed over the mountains on a trail which the Spaniards had supposed impassable, and, therefore, had not fortified or guarded; and the first they knew of the march of the American army was the appearance of a strong brigade within twenty miles of the northern coast, at the terminus of the railroad connecting San Juan with Arecibo.

The island of Puerto Rico was fairly won by the right of conquest and became a part of the United States. The sentiment of the people was in no sense outraged by the invaders, but, on the contrary, was successfully propitiated. A people who have endured the severity of Spanish rule for four centuries hail with joy the protection of the great republic. One of the richest sections of country over which our flag now floats has been added, and will be of lasting value to our nation politically, commercially, and from a military or strategic point of view. . . .

I remained in Puerto Rico as long as I deemed my presence necessary for carrying out the instructions of the President, and now return to the United States, bringing with me nearly five thousand men, who are no longer required, there being some twelve thousand still remaining, amply sufficient for all purposes.

There were but four real fights in the island, but the suspension of hostilities found conditions very favourable for several more, which would have taken place within a few hours: for General Brooke, who had been sent to accomplish the grand flank movement from Arroyo, had the mountain town of Cayey already under his guns; while General Wilson, who had advanced along the highway from Ponce, was firing briskly upon the intrenchments around Aybonito, with good prospect of their speedy capture. In the west, all the country between Ponce and Mayagüez was in our possession, and the latter city had been taken by General Schwan, who was advancing rapidly upon Aguadilla; while General Henry was striking northeasterly for Lares and Arecibo, which would have been ours without delay.

So the whole western and southern coast may be said to have been in our possession when orders were received to suspend firing; for, though hills and forests swarmed with Spanish soldiers, yet the gallant initiative of our troops at Santiago—never to retreat and to continually push forward—had its demoralizing effect upon the enemy. Theirs was a lost cause, also, and they knew it, fighting only in a faint-hearted manner and perfunctorily; for, as they would be marching out of a town at one side, while our troops were marching in at another, they could hear the native bands playing American airs, and cheering our flag and soldiers!

When, then, the brave boys were told by their general that they must "merely mark time a while," while the details of evacuation were arranged, and forego snatching the fruits of a victory that was almost within their grasp, it is no wonder that many strong men actually wept at their guns —as at Aybonito—and felt inclined to rebel.

They had gained their positions under perfect storms of bullets, which had stricken down their comrades on every side, and had unlimbered their guns while shell and shrapnel were screaming overhead; had just secured a position whence, as one of the gunners said, they could "sweep the Spaniards off the earth," when a superior power intervened, and saved the foe from annihilation. That they obeyed, though sullenly, and halted in their tracks, with guns loaded and trained upon the enemy, shows what admirable discipline prevailed among our volunteers and regulars.

It is a question whether our soldiers or the natives were the more disappointed, the former having been wrought up to fighting pitch, though without any malice or personal wrongs to avenge; the latter, still smarting under the recollection of many indignities, burning for revenge. But reason resumed its sway at last, and, with the exception of the atrocities committed by the Spanish soldiery at Ciàles, and the retributory punishment personally inflicted by the natives, there was no further fighting. In the hills, indeed, and on isolated plantations, bandit bands perpetrated atrocities, the society of the "Black Hand" extorting money by threats and murdering people indiscriminately.

The suspension of hostilities dates from the middle of August, 1898, and on the 16th the United States cruiser New Orleans entered the harbour of San Juan, which had been barred to our ships by mines and sunken wrecks hitherto, and the commander, Captain Folger, went ashore and paid his respects to Captain-General Macias, his call being returned the following day. Peace commissioners were appointed by the President of the United States, to meet and confer with those assigned to similar service by Spain, and on the last day of August, Rear-Admiral Schley and Brigadier-General Gordon sailed from New York, to meet the third commissioner, General Brooke, who was already in the island, and who advanced overland from his last position in front of the enemy to Rio Piedras and San Juan.

Six days later they met in the Capital, and were most courteously received by Captain-General Macias at a reception held in their honour at the palace, and mingled unreservedly, as friends, with those who but a short time previously were opposing them as bitter foes.

Hardly second in importance to the peace commissioners who were to arrange for the evacuation of the island were the postal commissioners, who sailed with them in the same ship. These were to follow after and gather up the threads dropped from military hands—in fact, our energetic Executive had already provided for the transmission of mails to and through the island, so far as practicable. The armistice afforded opportunity for establishing post offices well up to the front, and with the retirement of the Spanish soldiery and advance of our own, the postal service was carried along accordingly, until, with the evacuation by the Spaniards and occupation by the Americans, the insular system was already well established.

Thus had war and peace joined hands for the advancement of American ideas and promulgation of American methods. Almost without a jar—certainly without any appreciable shock to the natives —our officials were installed, our administration was established, and the confidence of our new colonists in our integrity perfectly won. So perfect was the *entente* between the American and Puerto Rican commissioners, so efficient the officials appointed for the purpose of promoting the evacuation, that by the first of October all details had been arranged, and by the eighteenth our Government was in possession, without friction, without disturbance, with every evidence of goodwill on both sides.

On the 18th of October, 1898, two cable despatches were sent from Puerto Rico to the United States. The first from San Juan de Puerto Rico:

Promptly at noon to-day the American flag was raised over San Juan. The ceremony was quiet and dignified, unmarred by disorder of any kind.

The Eleventh Regular Infantry, with two batteries of the Fifth Artillery, landed this morning. The latter proceeded to the fort, while the infantry lined up on the docks. It was a holiday for San Juan, and there were many people in the streets.

Rear-Admiral Schley and General Gordon, accompanied by their staffs, proceeded to the palace in carriages. The Eleventh Infantry and band, with Troop H of the Sixth United States Cavalry, then marched through the streets and formed in the square opposite the palace. At 11.40 A. M. General Brooke, Admiral Schley, and General Gordon, the United States Evacuation Commissioners, came out of the palace, with many naval officers, and formed on the right side of the square. The streets behind the soldiers were thronged with townspeople, who stood waiting in dead silence.

At last the city clock struck the hour of twelve, and the crowds, almost breathless, and with eyes fixed upon the flag pole, watched for developments. At the sound of the first gun from Fort Morro, Major Dean and Lieutenant Castle, of General Brooke's staff, hoisted the Stars and Stripes, while the band played the Star Spangled Banner.

All heads were bared and the crowds cheered. Fort Morro, Fort San Cristobal, and the United States revenue cutter Manning, lying in the harbor, fired twenty-one guns each.

Señor Munez Rivera, who was president of the recent Autonomist Council of Secretaries, and other officials of the late insular government, were present at the proceedings.

Congratulations and handshaking among the American officers followed. Ensign King hoisted the Stars and Stripes on the Intendencia, but all other flags on the various public buildings were hoisted by military officers. Simultaneously with the raising of the flag over the captain general's palace many others were hoisted in different parts of the city.

The second despatch from Ponce, Puerto Rico:

To-day's celebrations in connection with the formal surrender of the island of Puerto Rico were most enthusiastic. After the parade the bands and various trade organizations went to General Henry's headquarters. General Henry in a speech said:

"Alcalde and citizens: To-day the flag of the United States floats as an emblem of undisputed authority over the island of Puerto Rico, giving promise of protection to life, of liberty, prosperity, and the right to worship God in accordance with the dictates of conscience. The forty-five States represented by the stars emblazoned on the blue field of that flag unite in vouchsafing to you prosperity and protection as citizens of the American Union.

"Your future destiny rests largely with yourselves. Respect the rights of each other. Do not abuse the Government which accords opportunity to the individual for advancement. Political animosities must be forgotten in unity and in the recognition of common interests. I congratulate you all on beginning your public life under new auspices, free from governmental oppression, and with liberty to advance your own country's interests by your united efforts."

The Alcalde replied in part:

"We hope soon to see another star symbolic of our prosperity and of our membership in the great Republic of States. Puerto Rico has not accepted

Gathering cocoanuts.

American domination on account of force. She has suffered for many years the evils of error, neglect, and persecution, but she had men who studied the question of government, and who saw in America her redemption and a guarantee of life, liberty, and justice. There we came willingly and freely, hoping, hand in hand with the greatest of all republics, to advance in civilization and progress, and to become part of the Republic, to which we pledge our faith forever."

The town was profusely decorated with American flags.

A line of steamers has plied regularly between New York and Puerto Rico for many years, and, although until recently more devoted to freight than passenger traffic, it has been augmented so that the anticipated hegira to that island will be accommodated. In good weather the distance between New York and San Juan can be covered in four days, though the usual passage is five, and, as the waters beyond the Gulf Stream are generally smooth, a pleasurable voyage will be in prospect for those intending to visit this, our first acquisition in tropical American waters.

" The great outward pressure that all nations feel is the pressure of commerce for new markets; and statesmen, whether they know it or not, minister to trade, and through trade to civilization," says a talented writer in a contemporary magazine.

Not only as a prospectively valuable acquisition, for its as yet undeveloped resources, but as an actual factor in the world of commerce to-day, Puerto Rico holds out tempting allurements. By the last published statistics the island's foreign commerce aggregated $36,624,000 in 1896, exports and imports being pretty evenly divided. Spain, as the then "home country," received, of course, the largest share, or an average amount of $10,000,000; but the United States came next, with about $7,000,000, or twenty per cent.

Now, does it need a prophetic eye to foresee the result of the substitution of the United States for Spain, in the character of nurse or foster-mother? It may seem ungenerous to look this "gift-horse" in the mouth; but we may say, perhaps, without laying ourselves open to that charge, that, aside from the benefit directly resulting to the inhabitants of a territory which has hitherto had every incentive to industry suppressed by an alien soldiery and unsympathetic bureaucracy, there will be the advantage of *contiguity* of that country which is now destined to take their crude natural products and supply their demands for manufactured goods! In short, it would seem that the admission of the island of Puerto Rico within the Union might prove so mutually beneficial as to suggest the satisfying of that hiatus popularly known as a "long-felt want!" In anticipation of the fruit which this tropical tree, now shaken by northern blasts, is likely to yield, American investors followed swiftly after American soldiers, and it was estimated by one on the ground that at least three hundred of this class were in the province of Ponce alone before the details of evacuation had been completed.

Coincident with the announcement that Spanish authority had ceased, came word that the most important suburban tramway line of San Juan, that to Rio Piedras, had been transferred to American capitalists, who were to change the motive power from steam to electricity. The President of the United States was said to have been overwhelmed with applications for concessions and franchises, which he wisely declined to grant under the then existing conditions. A company was formed for the exploitation of the Antilles, with a capital of eighteen million dollars, even before peace was declared; transfers of landed properties were in process before the protocol was signed. Everywhere it was evident that our citizens were keenly alive to the fact that the first opportunity was now offered for acquiring tropical property protected by the Stars and Stripes.

While in the preceding pages the information set forth may already have anticipated the question (at least, that was the intention), still it may seem pertinent to inquire as to the opportunities offered in the island for the investment of capital. Prefacing his remarks with the well-known aphorism as to the fate of pioneers in general—that their bones whiten all the border lands of civilization, the writer would say that he does not feel competent to advise. In his statements as to the resources of Puerto Rico he has taken into account not alone the present resources, but the potential energies latent in the soil and vegetation. There is another Puerto Rico to arise from the ashes of the old—that is, American energy and capital will evoke wonders from the soil and convert the climate into an ally instead of an enemy. Hotels, sanatoriums, paradisaical winter resorts, will arise in the hills, and along the coast the lands will blossom with the products of every clime. That the island will become the chosen abiding place of wealth and culture during the colder months of the year, and that many an investor of small means will seek here a home for himself and family, we have every reason to believe.

There will be no winter to provide for; perpetual summer is no dream, but a reality; fuel is not needed, except for culinary purposes; clothing may be reduced to the minimum, and in the case of children to nothing at all; the house may be made without cost, and comfortable quarters provided by a few days' labour; food-plants are on every side; fowls of all kinds can be reared here, for they find a congenial home, multiply with astonishing rapidity, and, as there are no noxious reptiles or quadrupeds, like snakes and 'possums, they can be left to run wild and pick up their own living.

These are facts; it only remains for man to subordinate the works and products of Nature to his use. Nature is stubborn and unyielding; man is weak and a prey to fevers, as well as to melancholy and nostalgia. Can he live in the tropics and bear up against the combined effects of climate and isolation? Can he plant a *cafetal* or orangery, a cocoa wood or cacao grove, with a reasonable prospect of gathering its fruits, and of leaving it, a valuable possession, to his children?

According to an eminent savant of Europe, there is nothing in the equatorial climate, in the way of plagues or disease, that is not due to parasites, which may be found in almost all the climates of the earth, the difference being that in the tropical countries the bacilli thrive wonderfully under the favouring high temperature. Science is making rapid strides in the direction of successfully combating disease organisms, whether they be found in greater or less numbers, and it is not an overly venturesome opinion to say that the time is approaching when all the plagues of the earth will come under hygienic and medicinal control.

More than one scientific man has pointed out that the even temperatures of the tropical regions do not demand so hardy a constitution as is required by the long, cold winters, and the fierce hot summers of the so-called temperate zones, and it should not be forgotten that the hot climates of the earth were the original home of the whole human race!

Still, it is in the temperate regions that man has made his greatest development—in the arts, literature, science; in everything that makes for progress and well-being, and this is doubtless owing to the difference of environment. In the tropics his energies are dissipated; in the temperate zone he is thrown upon himself, as it were, and becomes resourceful, self-reliant.

In conclusion, we should note that the general opinion of those who have examined into the subject is, that Puerto Rico is not, in its strictest sense, a "poor man's country." While, if content to live as the natives live, a hand-to-mouth existence, he can easily gain a mere subsistence, yet the opportunities for expansion are not, at present, abounding. In other West Indian islands, notably in those belonging to the British, there are large tracts of so-called Crown lands, as well as abandoned estates, which may be obtained at low prices and on easy terms. But in Puerto Rico the Spanish Government had originally but little of that sort; and even if there were any, there is no doubt that the retiring officials will have lost no time in having it transferred to individual ownerships before the United States Government can bring it within its jurisdiction. Most of the "Crown" lands are those which have been seized in default of payment of taxes, and distributed among the favourites of the administration. That was the Spanish way of doing business, and it remains to be seen if a new and improved order will be introduced now that we are in possession.

Large tracts of sugar lands may be obtained, especially in the eastern districts of Humacao, Fajardo, and Guayama; but, even while sugar is not at present a profitable cultivation (except under conditions mentioned in the chapter on that subject), it is doubtful if lands can be acquired save by an immense expenditure, say of fifty thousand or one hundred thousand dollars. In a modified way the same holds true of the large coffee estates, which are held at about five hundred dollars per acre, though wild lands exist which should be available at not over twenty or thirty dollars per acre. The first comers, of course, will get the best lands; and, as in every other country, while many individuals will become impoverished in their adventures in this region, some again will acquire fortunes with but little effort. In a word, it will be here, as elsewhere, the "survival of the fittest"—that is to say, the keenest intelligence, the longest purse, and the shrewdest settler, will win in the end.

APPENDIX.

As the island of Puerto Rico, though for centuries a Spanish possession, is still *terra incognita* to most Americans it is believed that the following information, obtained from other sources than the author's personal observations, will prove of value in forming an estimate of its resources and in correcting any possible exuberance of fancy growing out of an intense interest in the subject.

The most flourishing plantations of Puerto Rico, says that invaluable publication, the Bulletin of the Bureau of the American Republics, for August, 1898, are situated on the littoral plains and in the valleys of rivers which, according to Longman's Gazetteer, are "intensely cultivated."

The principal products are sugar, molasses, coffee, tobacco; then maize, rice, cotton, hides, dye-woods, and timber. Coffee is produced to the extent of over 16,000 tons per annum, and the annual sugar production averages 67,000 tons.

The forests abound in mahogany, cedar, ebony, dyewoods, and a great variety of medicinal and industrial plants. All kinds of tropical fruits are found. An average of 190,000,000 bananas, 6,500,-000 oranges, 2,500,000 cocoanuts, and 7,000,000 pounds of tobacco is produced annually.

Sugar-cane is cultivated on 61,000 acres, the districts in which it is produced on the largest scale being Ponce, 6,500 acres; Juana Diaz, 4,000 acres; Vieques, 3,000; Arecibo, 3,000; San Germán, 2,500. Coffee is cultivated on about 122,000 acres, two thirds of the whole being in the following districts: Utuado, Las Marias, Adjuntas, Maricao, Ponce, Lares, Mayagüez, Yauco, San Sebastian, Ciales, Barros, and Juan Diaz. Ponce, Mayagüez, and Arecibo are the provinces which produce more largely than any others in the island. It is estimated that every acre of coffee plantation averages in production 330 pounds. Tobacco is cultivated on over 2,000 acres, and over 1,100,000 acres are devoted to pastures. As these figures change from year to year they can be given only approximately. The total quantity of "declared lands" in 1894 amounted to 3,171 square miles, and as the total extent of the island of Puerto Rico is some 3,668 square miles, the difference between the rural property and the total area is 497 square miles, which are taken up by the towns, roads, rivers, bays, etc.

The sugar industry, until within the past few years, has been the most important, but, owing to the excessive land tax assessed by the Spanish officials and the growing use of beet sugar, it has in later years suffered a marked decline. Then, too, most of the mills used are equipped with machinery of an obsolete character. All the natural conditions—soil, climate, and labour—are favourable to the culture of this product, and it will no doubt now revive and flourish to an extent hitherto unknown.

Coffee is also a staple product. The greater part of it was formerly shipped to New York, where it commanded a good price. Much of the coffee now produced is grown by planters of small capital, who make use of the wild and waste lands of the hillsides to grow the berry. They prefer to cultivate coffee on account of the ease with which it can be produced, requiring but little expenditure as compared with the manufacture of sugar and molasses.

Tobacco, which ranks second in quality to that of Cuba, can be produced in great quantities, but the natives are generally careless in guarding against destructive insects and in drying and sorting the leaves. A considerable quantity, both in the form of leaf and manufactured cigars, is exported each year to the United States, England, France, Cuba, and Spain. Three qualities are produced: *Capa*, which is the leaf of first quality, used for wrappers; *tripa*, also a wrapper of medium grade; and *beliche*, or ordinary leaf. Tobacco culture is capable of enormous development here under favourable circumstances.

A small quantity of cacao is produced each year. Maize is grown on considerable areas only at times when high prices promise to prevail. Some cotton is also produced. Grass grows luxuriantly and affords pasturage for numerous herds of cattle, nearly all of which are exported. The hides of those consumed on the island are sent to other countries.

The mineral resources are not very extensive. Gold is found in limited quantities. Some copper, lead, iron, and coal are obtained. Lignite and yellow amber are found at Utuado and Moca. There are undeveloped resources of marble, limestone, and other building stone. The salt works at Guanica, Salinas, and Cape Rojo are under governmental control. Hot springs and mineral waters are found at Coamo, Juana Diaz, San Sebastian, San Lorenzo, and Ponce. The first-named are the most noted.

246   PUERTO RICO AND ITS RESOURCES.

LAND AND MINING LAWS.

There is no public land in the island of Puerto Rico, therefore colonization must be undertaken there, as in Cuba, by private enterprise. The population of Puerto Rico is very dense, and all the land has been taken. The royal ordinance of colonization and the *Ley de Extrangeria* (statute on aliens) do not grant concessions of land or offer any material inducement to immigration. Cuba and Puerto Rico have not, therefore, any law tending to encourage foreign immigration, as is the case in most of the American countries; and although foreigners are welcomed and their rights protected by law, no especial privileges are granted for settlement in those islands. The mining law in force in Puerto Rico is the same as that of Cuba. After the mineral is found, titles may be obtained by applying to the civil government where the mine is located. In case the mine is situated on private land, forcible expropriation may be obtained, the corresponding indemnity having been paid.

MANUFACTURES.

But little manufacturing is carried on. The Standard Oil Company has a small refinery across the bay from San Juan, at which crude petroleum brought from the United States is rectified. Sugar making is the chief industry. At San Juan matches, ice, soap, and a cheap variety of travelling cases are manufactured; there are also tanneries and foundries in the island.

POLITICAL DIVISIONS AND GOVERNMENT.

The island is divided into seven districts, and under Spanish sovereignty its affairs were administered by a captain-general, who was the civil as well

APPENDIX. 247

as the military executive, appointed by the Crown, with representation in the Spanish Cortes or Parliament. In 1897, through a royal decree, the island was granted autonomous government, with a colonial parliament, the executive power being vested in a governor-general, with department secretaries. Under the agreement with Spain for the conclusion of peace, Puerto Rico is ceded to the United States, and, for the present (1898), is governed by the military commanders under the instructions of the United States War Department.

TRANSPORTATION FACILITIES.

One of the greatest drawbacks in this really wonderful island has been the lack of adequate transportation facilities. All the roads, except the main government road, are of the most primitive sort and are quite impassable during the rainy seasons. The "consumption tax" on liquors and petroleum has been ceded to the municipalities, the last few years, to be used in repairing the highways. According to the latest available reports, the total length of finished railroads is about 136 miles, with 170 miles under construction. Lines connect San Juan and Camuy, Aguadilla and Mayagüez, Yauco and Ponce, Carolina and San Juan, San Juan and Rio Pedras, and San Juan and Catana. The New York Commercial Advertiser of August 13, 1898, gives a full account of the railroads, written by a resident, as follows:

"Mail, telegraph, and railroad communications are of such a kind that should they disappear entirely the people could do just as well without them. It is only since the year 1878 that railroads have been known in Puerto Rico, and since then the country has advanced very little. There are only three railroad lines in the whole island, covering in all one hundred and thirty-six miles. The first one was opened in 1878, the East Railroad Line, from San Juan to Rio Piedras, a distance of six miles and a quarter, covered in fifty-five minutes, making several stops of one or two minutes. The fare is thirty cents from San Juan to Rio Piedras, or five cents per mile, and between San Juan or Rio Piedras and the intermediate stations the rate is about the same. This is the best managed line on the island, and runs twelve trains daily, with comfortable and quite elegant cars, although it may be noticed that the speed is limited.

"The West Railroad Line, opened in 1881, from San Juan to Catano, crosses the harbour by ferryboat, and thence to Bayamon by a so-called train. This line is the worst thing imaginable, and would furnish plenty of material for a book on railroad mismanagement. Trains are run every two and three hours, and the trip from San Juan to Bayamon, or *vice versa*, a distance of six miles, is supposed to be made in an hour, but this has never been done. It always takes an hour and a quarter at least, even barring accidents, which are quite numerous, owing to the fact that there are only two engines and two boats, all in a very poor condition.

"This line issues tickets from San Juan to Bayamon, connecting at that point with the Arecibo train; very often the West Railroad train is late, the passenger misses the Arecibo one, and, as there is only a daily train, has to wait till next day at his own expense. Civil or criminal suits are never brought against any railroad, as the plaintiff is quite sure to have judgment rendered against him.

"Both these lines are owned by private individuals, so the Government is not to blame for their poor management, except for allowing them to violate all rules.

APPENDIX. 249

"The longest road in the island is the 'Circumvallation Railroad,' and here the way things are done by the Spanish Government can be better judged. In almost every country railroad companies pay taxes, but in Puerto Rico things are quite different. This railroad is owned by a French Company, to which the Government guarantees an eight per cent profit on the capital invested. Under this contract it is easy to imagine that the management is very poor; the company never makes the eight per cent stipulated, and the country has to pay for something that does not benefit the people, as few can use the railroad owing to its high rates.

"This contract was made in Madrid, the interests of the Puerto Rico people not being considered at all. Although the construction of this railroad was begun in 1887, and the company agreed to complete it in ten years, up to the present time only one third of it is in operation, and nobody can tell when the remainder will be finished. . . .

"The particular feature of this railroad is that fares must be paid, not in Puerto Rico provincial coin, but in Spanish currency, with a premium that has been increasing for the last three years, reaching thirty and thirty-five per cent. On this account the passenger never knows how much the ticket will be till he reaches the station and reads on the slate the rate of exchange. That, as a rule, is as high as possible, for there is very little Spanish coin in the island, and the public has to pay what the company asks."

CUSTOMS TARIFF AND SHIPPING REGULATIONS.

The customs tariff for Puerto Rico was promulgated by the War Department of the United States on the 19th of August. The rates applied are those of the minimum tariff formerly imposed by Spain. Under Spanish sovereignty, United States products entering Puerto Rico paid the maximum rates. They are now on an equal footing with those of other nations.

The tonnage and landing charges are practically the same as provided in the Cuban regulations, but speaking generally, the customs duties are lower. The Spanish tax of fifty cents on each ton of merchandise landed at San Juan and Mayagüez for harbour improvements is continued. The following articles are admitted free:

Trees, plants, and moss in a natural or fresh state.

Gold and silver ores.

Samples of felt, painted paper, and tissues, when they comply with specified conditions.

Samples of trimmings in small pieces of no commercial value or possible application.

Gold, silver, and platinum, in broken-up jewelry or table services, bars, sheets, coins, pieces, dust, and scrap.

Also the following under conditions:

Natural manures and guano.

National products returning from foreign exhibits, on presentation of the bill of lading or certificate proving their exportation from the island and of satisfactory evidence attesting that such products have been presented and have been shipped to their point of departure.

Wearing apparel, toilet objects, and articles for personal use, bed and table linen, books, portable tools and instruments, theatrical costumes, jewels, and table services bearing evident signs of having been used, imported by travellers in their luggage in quantities proportioned to their class, profession, and position.

APPENDIX. 251

When travellers do not bring their baggage with them, the clearing of the same may be made by the conductor or persons authorized for the purpose, provided that they prove to the satisfaction of the customs officers that the effects are destined for private use.

Works of fine art acquired by the Government, academies, or other official corporations, and destined for museums, galleries, or art schools, when due proof is given as to their destination.

Archæological and numismatical objects for public museums, academies, and scientific and artistic corporations on proof of their destination.

Specimens and collections of mineralogy and botany, and small models for public museums, schools, academies, and scientific and artistic corporations, on proof of their destination.

Receptacles which have been shipped from the island with fruit, sugar, molasses, and spirits, and which are reimported empty, including receptacles known as "pipotes," of galvanized iron, intended for the exportation of alcohol.

Carriages, trained animals, portable theatres, panoramas, wax figures, and other similar objects for public entertainment, imported temporarily, provided bond be given.

Used furniture of persons coming to settle in the island.

Foreign articles coming to exhibitions held in the island.

Submarine telegraph cables.

Pumps intended exclusively for the salvage of vessels.

Parts of machinery, pieces of metal, and wood imported for the repair of foreign and national vessels which have entered ports in the islands through stress of weather.

252   PUERTO RICO AND ITS RESOURCES.

THE NAVIGATION RULES

Applying to Puerto Rico are stated in the following order of the United States Commissioner of Navigation.

Clearance of Vessels to Cuba and Puerto Rico.

TREASURY DEPARTMENT, BUREAU OF NAVIGATION,
WASHINGTON, D. C., *August 15, 1898.*

To Collectors of Customs and Others:

Vessels may clear to ports in Cuba and Puerto Rico, subject to the laws and regulations in force relating to clearances, except that vessels of the United States only will be cleared for the transportation of merchandise in the trade between the United States and Puerto Rico.

Approved:
L. G. GAGE, *Secretary.*

T. B. SANDERS,
Acting Commissioner.

While only United States vessels may be cleared for Puerto Rico, it is understood that foreign vessels touching at United States ports will be permitted to proceed to Puerto Rico.

POSTAL RATES.

The following order of the Postmaster-General of the United States establishes regulations which will doubtless apply to the whole of the island of Puerto Rico:

Civilians' Mail for and from Ponce, Puerto Rico.

POST-OFFICE DEPARTMENT,
WASHINGTON, D. C., *August 2, 1898.*

ORDER No. 319.

In conformity with the order of the President of the 21st ultimo, my order (No. 161) of the 26th of

APPENDIX. 253

April last, prohibiting the despatch of any mail matter to Spain or her dependencies, is modified so far as to permit postal communication between the United States and Ponce, Puerto Rico.

The mails sent to Ponce may contain mail matter of all classes allowable in the domestic mails of the United States, addressed for delivery at any place within the territory occupied by the United States forces in the vicinity of Ponce; and the mails sent from Ponce may contain the same classes of mail matter addressed for delivery in the United States, all articles included in said mails being subject to inspection by the proper military or naval authorities.

The postal rates applicable to articles originating in or destined for the United States in the mails in question are fixed as follows, viz.:

First-class matter, five cents per half ounce.

Postal cards, single, two cents; double, four cents.

Second- and third-class matter, one cent for each two ounces.

Fourth-class matter, one cent for each ounce.

Registration fee, eight cents.

Only United States postage stamps will be valid for the prepayment of postage. Prepayment shall not be required, but if postage is not prepaid in full, double the amount of the deficient postage at the above rates shall be collected on delivery to addresses in the United States or Puerto Rico.

To articles originating in or destined for countries beyond the United States, the Postal Union rates and conditions shall apply.

The mails for Ponce must be addressed to the United States postal agent at Ponce, and the delivery of any article may be withheld if deemed necessary by the proper military or naval authorities.

Compensation to merchant vessels for the sea

conveyance of mails from Ponce shall be made at the rates heretofore paid to merchant vessels for conveying mails from the United States to Ponce.

CHARLES EMORY SMITH,
Postmaster-General.

BANKING AND CURRENCY, WEIGHTS AND MEASURES.

There is a bank at San Juan, the capital, with branches at the principal points in the islands. Mexican money was current until the end of 1895, when a five-peseta piece was coined and put in circulation.

The metric system of weights and measures is in use in Puerto Rico.

It should be noted that both the customs and postal regulations are subject to revision and change, in view of the present inchoate condition of affairs, and should not be accepted as final.

TRADE OF PUERTO RICO.

Valuable statistics respecting the trade of Puerto Rico were gathered by Mr. F. H. Hitchcock, Chief of Foreign Markets, United States Department of Agriculture, and published in July, 1898.

"Following is a summary statement of the imports and exports of Puerto Rico during each calendar year from 1887 to 1896, inclusive. The original values in *pesos*, as published in the official returns of trade issued by the Puerto Rican customs authorities, are accompanied by their nominal equivalent in United States dollars. The figures are as follows:

APPENDIX. 255

Value of Merchandise * imported and exported by Puerto Rico during Each Calendar Year from 1887 to 1896, Inclusive.

Calendar Years.	Imports.		Exports.†		Total imports and exports.	Excess of imports (+) or exports (−).
	Pesos.	Dollars.	Pesos.	Dollars.	Dollars.	Dollars.
1887	11,012,964	10,627,510	10,994,913	10,610,091	21,237,601	+ 17,419
1888	14,389,673	13,886,034	11,999,255	11,579,281	25,465,315	+ 2,306,753
1889	14,177,577	13,681,362	11,066,684	10,679,350	24,360,712	+ 3,002,012
1890	18,230,385	17,592,322	10,710,519	10,335,651	27,927,973	+ 7,256,671
1891	16,864,764	16,274,497	9,885,999	9,539,989	25,814,486	+ 6,734,508
Annual average, 1887–1891	14,935,073	14,412,345	10,931,474	10,548,872	24,961,217	+ 3,863,473
1892	17,081,610	16,483,754	16,076,312	15,513,641	31,997,395	+ 970,113
1893	17,320,454	16,714,238	16,745,393	16,159,304	32,873,542	+ 554,934
1894	19,778,587	19,086,336	17,295,535	16,690,191	35,776,527	+ 2,396,145
1895	17,446,065	16,835,453	15,798,590	15,245,639	32,081,092	+ 1,589,814
1896	18,945,793	18,282,690	19,006,663	18,341,430	36,624,120	− 58,740
Annual average, 1892–1896	18,114,502	17,480,494	16,984,499	16,390,041	33,870,535	+ 1,090,453

* Not including coin and bullion. † Including re-exports.

Trade of Puerto Rico by Countries.

"The foreign trade of Puerto Rico is conducted chiefly with Spain, the United States, Cuba, Germany, the United Kingdom, and France. Of all the merchandise imported and exported by the island during the four years 1893-1896, fully eighty-five per cent, measured in value, was exchanged with the six countries mentioned. Spain received the largest share of the trade, the transactions with that country in 1893-1896, according to the Puerto Rican statistics, having an average annual value of $9,888,074, which was 28.80 per cent of the total valuation placed upon the island's commerce. The United States, as a participator in the trade, ranked second only to Spain, the value of the goods exchanged averaging $6,845,252 a year, or 19.94 per cent of the total. After Spain and the United States, Cuba was the most important factor, the proportion of the trade credited to that island amounting to 13.41 per cent, and having an average yearly value of $4,606,-220. Spain, the United States, and Cuba together enjoyed nearly two thirds of the total commerce carried on by Puerto Rico during 1893-1896. About one fourth of the trade was controlled by three European countries—Germany, the United Kingdom, and France. The average value per annum of the business transacted with Germany in the four years mentioned amounted to $3,050,334, or 8.88 per cent of the total; that with the United Kingdom to $2,863,-930, or 8.34 per cent; and that with France to $2,201,687, or 6.41 per cent."

APPENDIX.

Value of Merchandise* imported and exported by the United States in Our Trade with Puerto Rico during Each Fiscal Year from 1888 to 1897, Inclusive.

YEARS ENDED JUNE 30—	IMPORTS.			EXPORTS.			Total imports and exports.	Excess of imports (+) or exports (—).
	Free.	Dutiable.	Total.	Domestic merchandise.	Foreign merchandise.	Total.		
1888	$293,450	$4,119,033	$4,412,483	$1,920,358	$49,260	$1,969,618	$6,382,101	+ $2,442,865
1889	103,720	3,603,653	3,707,373	2,175,458	49,473	2,224,931	5,932,304	+ 1,482,442
1890	176,394	3,877,232	4,053,626	2,247,700	49,838	2,297,538	6,351,164	+ 1,756,088
1891	1,856,955	1,307,155	3,164,110	2,112,334	42,900	2,155,234	5,319,344	+ 1,008,876
1892	3,236,337	11,670	3,248,007	2,808,631	47,372	2,856,003	6,104,010	+ 392,004
Annual average, 1888–'92	$1,133,371	$2,583,749	$3,717,120	$2,252,896	$47,769	$2,300,665	$6,017,785	+ $1,416,455
1893	$3,994,673	$13,950	$4,008,623	$2,502,788	$7,819	$2,510,607	$6,519,230	+ $1,498,016
1894	3,126,895	8,739	3,135,634	2,705,646	14,862	2,720,508	5,856,142	+ 415,126
1895	375,364	1,131,148	1,506,512	1,820,203	13,341	1,833,544	3,340,056	— 327,032
1896	48,608	2,248,045	2,296,653	2,080,400	21,694	2,102,094	4,398,747	+ 194,559
1897	101,711	2,079,313	2,181,024	1,964,850	24,038	1,988,888	4,169,912	+ 192,136
Annual average, 1893–'97	$1,529,450	$1,096,239	$2,625,689	$2,214,777	$16,351	$2,231,128	$4,856,817	+ $394,561

* Not including gold and silver coin and bullion.

Temperature and Rainfall.

From Bulletin No. 22, United States Department of Agriculture, Weather Bureau, the Following Data were obtained:

SAN JUAN, PUERTO RICO (12 Years).

	Jan	Feb	Mar	Apr	May	Jun	Jul	Aug	Sep	Oct	Nov	Dec
Temperature (Fahr.):												
Mean	76.6	75.7	76.6	77.9	79.3	81.5	81.1	81.3	81.0	80.6	79.2	76.5
Highest	93.2	92.5	95.4	95.0	100.8	99.9	96.8	99.0	96.8	97.9	99.1	92.5
Lowest	57.2	58.3	60.1	60.8	62.6	64.8	64.0	64.0	64.9	61.2	59.4	56.1
Rainfall:												
Mean	2.28	1.80	2.07	5.35	6.38	5.96	5.82	6.21	5.83	5.63	7.62	3.88
Greatest	8.60	5.26	12.40	11.78	12.25	8.91	11.58	17.07	10.00	11.98	11.73	6.34
Least	1.07	0.35	0.29	1.61	1.90	2.34	2.48	3.04	2.91	1.97	3.40	1.90

Year
78.9
100.8
56.1
59.45
82.64
45.79

"In the island of Jamaica the rainy season appears to begin in May and ends, as at Havana, in October. At Port au Prince, Haiti, and San Juan, Puerto Rico, it begins in April and ends at the former in October and at the latter in November, while in the island of St. Thomas, to the east of Puerto Rico, the rainy season appears to be embraced in the months of October, November, and December; also in other islands of the Lesser Antilles irregularities are observed."

Live Stock of the Island.

From the official statistics of Puerto Rico we learn that the number of cattle and domestic animals of all kinds on the island in October, 1896, was:

Horses	65,751 head
Oxen and cows	303,612 "
Mules	4,467 "
Asses	717 "
Sheep	2,055 "
Goats	5,779 "
Swine	13,411 "

As a Winter Resort.

"As a delightful winter resort, a valuable tropical garden, and an important strategic point, Puerto Rico is an invaluable acquisition to the people and Government of the United States."

This is the opinion of Mr. O. P. Austin, Chief of the Treasury Bureau of Statistics at Washington, a trained observer, an expert statistician, and an author of note, who made a flying trip to Puerto Rico in September, 1898.

"But it must not be expected," continued Mr. Austin, "that so small an island can become a large factor in supplying the $250,000,000 worth of tropical productions which the people of the United States annually consume, or that it can absorb a very large percentage of the $1,200,000,000 worth of our annual productions. Smaller in area than the State of Connecticut and with a population less than that of the city of Brooklyn, it may not be able to meet the somewhat extravagant expectations which enthusiastic people have formed with reference to it. Settled by Spain more than a century earlier than the landing of the Pilgrims at Plymouth Rock, its population is now more dense than that of Massachusetts, and the prospect of materially increasing its productiveness is not flattering. Mountainous from centre to circumference, the nearly 1,000,000 people who occupy its 3,700 square miles of territory have put under cultivation most of the available soil, and while their methods of culture and transportation are in many cases very primitive, it can not be expected that the productions of this densely populated and closely cultivated area can be largely increased or its consumption greatly multiplied.

"The valleys and coast lands are well occupied with sugar estates, the area adjoining these is devoted to tobacco, and the mountain sides to the very peaks are occupied by large coffee plantations, with patches of cocoanuts, bananas, plantains, breadfruit, oranges, and other tropical fruits scattered among them. While the two hundred thousand of its population who live in cities and villages enjoy some of the conveniences to which our people are accustomed, the large proportion of the rural population is of extremely simple habits in the matter of food, clothing, and habitation, and, with small earning capacity and a small per capita of a depreciated currency, can not be expected to soon become large consumers of our products. A little rice, a very little flour, a few beans, and plenty of bananas, plantains, bread-fruit, and vegetables satisfy their physical necessities; a few yards of cotton cloth for the adults and nothing for the children meet their principal requirements for clothing; while a few rough boards and a plentiful supply of plaintain and palm leaves supply the material for the humble dwellings throughout the interior and in many of the villages. With but about one fifth of its population able to read and write, the knowledge of the outside world is extremely limited, and with only one hundred and fifty miles of railroad and less than two hundred and fifty miles of good wagon road on the island the means of intercommunication are not such as to enable a prompt stimulation of its production or consumption. Most of the good roads (and some of them are very fine) run from town to town along the coast, though there is one exception in the military road connecting Ponce on the south shore with San Juan on the north shore. Most of the interior, however, is only reached by bridle paths, over which transportation is effected by packs carried on small ponies. In the cities and towns most of the transportation is by bullocks yoked in primitive fashion to two-wheeled carts and urged to their work by a sharp pointed pole in the hands of a native driver, who walks in front of his team, turning to give them a vigorous punch when they do not follow with sufficient speed. The cattle of the island are of a superior class, similar in appearance to the Jersey cattle, but with broad horns, the cows being driven from door to door in the towns and milked into bottles in the presence of the customer, while the calves stand patiently upon the sidewalk awaiting the removal of the peripatetic dairy to the residence of the next customer.

"Education on the island is not of a very high order. A sort of public-school system prevails in some of the towns and cities, but in the interior reading and writing, except among the plantation owners and managers, are rare. Spanish is the popular tongue, though the natives of France, of whom there are quite a number, retain their language, and there are in the towns some English-speaking negroes from St. Thomas and other nearby colonies, who prove useful as interpreters to the Americans already on the island. One of the two daily newspapers published in Ponce prints one page in English, out of compliment to the new conditions, most of the matter so published being extracts from the Constitution of the United States and sketches of the lives of our distinguished men. There are Catholic churches in all the cities and large towns, some of them dating back over a century, handsomely finished within and representing a large expenditure of money. There is one Protestant church in Ponce, said to have been the only one in the Spanish West Indies, but it is at present unoccupied. There are theatres in the principal cities, and several of the leading towns have telephones and are connected by telegraph lines aggregating about four hundred miles in length, while cable communication is had with the United States at $1.17 per word.

"The currency and finances of the island are subjects with which our statesmen will have to deal. The Spanish Government in 1895 took up all the Mexican and Spanish coins in circulation and substituted special silver coins struck in the mint of Spain for this purpose. They bear on one side the Spanish coat of arms and the words 'Isla de Puerto Rico,' and on the other the face of the boy king and an elaborate inscription in Spanish. The largest of these is the *peso*, of one hundred centavos, corresponding in appearance with our silver dollars, weighing 385.5 grains, and generally spoken of as a 'dollar.' There are also smaller silver coins of five, ten, twenty, and forty centavos, the twenty-centavo piece being known as the *peseta*, also copper coins of one and two centavos. The Spanish Government makes no attempt to maintain the standing of these silver coins, and they represent little more than their bullion value, the banks and merchants gladly exchanging $1.75 in this coin for one dollar in our silver or paper, and exchanges being sometimes made at two for one, and even higher. The native drivers, boatmen, and venders have already learned the superior value of our coins, and a twenty-five cent piece in United States coin is readily accepted at from forty-five to fifty cents in payment for their services. That it will be necessary to take up this fluctuating coin when our permanent measure of value permeates this island is generally conceded, but just what plan should be adopted in fixing the rate at which obligations made in Puerto Rican coin shall be paid in that of the United States is a matter for statesmen to determine. Another interesting question in this connection is whether or not the plantation labour which has in the past been satisfied with fifty to sixty cents per day in Puerto Rican money will be content to accept twenty-five to thirty cents per day in our coins in its stead. The silver money coined and sent to the island by Spain amounted to six million dollars or pesos, and there has been added about one million in paper by certain of the five banks of the island, some of which stands at par with the silver and some at a discount, but it is seldom seen in ordinary business transactions. The fact that our own Government has just sent in a shipment to the island a sum equal in value to one tenth of the entire currency, and that it will be immediately put into circulation through its payment to the troops scattered over the island, furnishes a suggestion as to the probable increase of the currency and increased disparity in value! Statistically the productions and commerce of Puerto Rico have been already discussed. The exports amount to about $15,000,000 a year gold value, and the imports about $16,000,000. Coffee forms about 60 per cent of the value of the exports, sugar 20 per cent, tobacco 5 per cent, and the remainder made up of cacao, rum, hides, sponges, cabinet, woods, etc. Practically all the coffee goes to Europe, the grocers and dealers asserting that they can obtain higher prices, especially for the fine grades, which rank with Java and Mocha, in France and Spain than in the United States, while the fact that the export duty on coffee, tobacco, and cattle was only one tenth as much on articles sent to Spain as on those sent to other countries encouraged exporters to send their goods to Spanish ports. Of the importations, about 50 per cent are manufactured articles, largely cotton cloths, shoes, fancy goods, and articles of household use, 15 per cent rice, 10 per cent fish, 10 per cent meats and lard, and 7 per cent flour. Naturally, most of this came from Spain, because the duty collected on articles from that country was only one tenth of that on articles from other countries. While considerable sums are collected from the tariff, the Spanish Government also collected a large amount by other methods, dealers and property owners being required to pay to the Spanish Government one half as much tax as was collected for the local government, whose expenses were high, thus making the tax burden very heavy.

"Much interest is already being evinced by people from the United States in the matter of investments in Puerto Rico, and on this subject there is a variety of opinion. Coffee plantations are first considered, as they have a reputation of having paid from 15 to

25 per cent profit annually upon their cost. They are held at high prices, however, from $75 to $200 per acre in Puerto Rican money, according to location, quality of coffee produced, age of trees, etc. The western part of the island is considered the best for coffee, and produces the celebrated *Café Caracolilla*, which is all sent to Europe at the export price of thirty-two cents per pound in Puerto Rican money. Sugar plantations are considered next in importance, and are relatively higher in price because of the more expensive machinery required, while their attractiveness as investments is reduced by the fact that many plantations have of late been abandoned as such and turned into cattle ranges. Tobacco has been very profitable of late because of the shortage in Cuban tobacco, for which it has been substituted, though whether it will continue its popularity when the Cuban article resumes its normal position in the market is uncertain. Tropical fruits have had little attention, either among local exporters or American investors, but might prove more profitable than the other interests more discussed, as they are ready for shipment at a time of the year when the markets of the United States have not begun receiving the Florida or California fruits. As to the increase which may be expected in the production and consumption of the island, it will depend somewhat upon the improvements made in harbours, roads, transportation facilities, etc., and the energy with which the Americans may push the work of its development. The land in the valleys is extremely rich, and that of the mountain sides, even to the very top, is of good colour and productive, especially for coffee and some of the fruits. With the opening of roads to the interior it is probable that considerable land not now tilled would be brought under cultivation, and the general concensus of opinion among intelligent resi-

dents of the island is that the products can be increased fifty per cent, or perhaps more, and the profit greatly increased by modern methods of cultivation and transportation, and the consuming power of the island increased in about the same proportion. Even should this happen, however, the island could furnish but about ten per cent of our annual consumption of tropical products, and consume but about two per cent of our annual exports. The business enterprises most likely to be successful in Puerto Rico are those related to the tropical productions which flourish there and can not flourish in the United States, while to our own temperate climate and well-established industries should be left the task of supplying the general food products and manufactures required by the people there, sending them the products of our grain fields and factories by the vessels which return laden with their tropical growths. An acre of land in Puerto Rico can produce more of value in sugar, or coffee, or tobacco, or fruit than if planted in corn or potatoes or used as pasture, while there are single counties in the United States larger than all Puerto Rico which are only suitable for the production of these general food supplies. While there is a general demand for manufactures in Puerto Rico, they can be more cheaply supplied by our great factories at home than to attempt their manufacture there, especially as no coal has yet been developed in the island, and fuel is high and water power not to be relied upon. Ice factories and breweries would probably do well there, and it is believed that the production of grapes and the manufacture of wine would be successful, while the cigar industry would be profitable with the plentiful native labour and high grade tobacco, especially if all tariff restrictions upon trade between the island and the United States shall be removed.

APPENDIX. 267

Among the most important needs for the development of the island are a thorough survey and readjustment of property lines and titles, construction of roads and harbour facilities, and the establishment of such hotel enterprises as will make practicable a leisurely and careful study of its conditions—conditions which have never been carefully studied or developed by the Spanish Government, which has controlled the island since 1509.

"As a resort for pleasure seekers or those desiring a delightful winter climate, Puerto Rico will be very attractive so soon as direct and fast steamship lines and American hotels supply some of the comforts to which the people of the United States have become accustomed. The constant breeze from the sea by day and the land at night renders the climate a fairly comfortable one even in August, and the opportunity to obtain almost any desired altitude, coupled with the mineral springs which are said to abound, will make the island attractive to those seeking health as well as recreation.

"In the cities and towns the succession of strange sights and sounds presents a kaleidoscopic and always interesting spectacle. The street venders, carrying their stores upon their heads or in huge panniers upon diminutive ponies, announce their wares in strange and not unmusical cries, long lines of rude carts drawn by broad horned bullocks crowd the streets, native women smoking black cigars flit hither and thither, nude children of all colours and ages below eight disport themselves unconcernedly upon the sidewalks and streets, while soldiers and officers are everywhere, busy with their duties establishing order and new conditions. On the country roads the succession of mountains and valleys covered with tropical growth, dashing mountain streams and overhanging cliffs, and the large sugar and coffee plantations dotted with the tiny houses of their native workmen, present a panorama of constant interest.

"Puerto Rico now resumes, politically, the relations with this continent which long ago existed physically. Torn by great natural movements from the mainland of which this chain of islands doubtless formed a part, she is now restored by another great natural movement which is reuniting the continents and countries and islands in a system of republics having one great purpose of co-operation and mutual advancement. Alone she can furnish but a small part of the tropical supplies for which we have been accustomed to send two hundred and fifty million dollars abroad each year, but with the co-operation of undeveloped Cuba, Hawaii, and the Philippines, should they fall within our borders, would enable us to expend among our own people practically all of that vast sum which we have heretofore been compelled to send to foreign lands and foreign people."

ADVICE TO IMMIGRANTS.

The following report from Mr. Hanna, former American Consul at Puerto Rico, was received by the Assistant Secretary of State, and will be of interest to persons contemplating migration to that island. In this report Mr. Hanna says:

"I am convinced that young men seeking work or positions of any kind should not come to Puerto Rico. Such persons as clerks, carpenters, mechanics, and labourers of all grades should stay away. No American should come to Puerto Rico expecting to 'strike it rich,' and no persons should come here without plenty of money to pay board bills and have enough to take them back to their homes in the United States. This is a small island, has

APPENDIX. 269

a population of about a million people (?), and is the most densely populated country in the world. There are several hundred thousand working Puerto Ricans ready to fill the vacant jobs and at a low price. There may come a time, after the laws of the United States are applied by Congress to this island, that this will be a good place for American capital and for Americans to do business, but even then a man should have plenty of money who expects to make a business success in Puerto Rico. I deem it important that the Department cause this suggestion to be made public through the newspapers of the country."

FROM THE LONDON TIMES.

" There is no room for doubt that the more educated portion of the population who are possessors of real estate or other property in Puerto Rico appreciate that the change in ownership of the island is to their material benefit. It is also necessary to bear in mind that the Puerto Rican has always been treated by the Spaniard as belonging to an inferior caste, and the knowledge of this fact has been most galling to the inhabitants here. Moreover, such treatment has not been justified by circumstances, a considerable number of the more wealthy families of the island being fully equal in refinement, culture, and general intelligence to the most aristocratic representatives and officials sent to this country from Madrid.

" In so far as the Spaniards engaged in commerce are concerned, I think they regard the change of government with equanimity. Spanish merchants in these countries are generally keen business men, who do not allow their patriotism to interfere with their pockets, and they quite realize that in the present instance their interests and rights will be fully protected. An increase in the volume of business to be transacted will go far toward palliating any harsh feelings that may exist to-day as the result of the recent occurrences, and the United States Government need have small reason to fear that the Spaniards who remain in the island will prove other than law-abiding and industrious citizens.

"As regards foreign residents generally, there can be no question that they will be better off under United States than under Spanish rule. They will enjoy sounder security for life and property than has hitherto been the case; they will have a legal remedy in disputes connected with commercial transactions or other matters where they are unjustly treated— a remedy which the intricacies of the Spanish courts have debarred the great majority of injured persons from appealing to in the past.

"But with the mass of the native inhabitants other considerations crop up, and trouble may occur in consequence. Among the seven hundred thousand people comprising the lower class of the population of Puerto Rico the code of morality is of a very low order. Respect for law and order has never been rigidly enforced by the Spanish authorities, and this leniency has resulted in a license as to all moral obligations becoming almost an ingrained part of the native character.

"From the observations I have made in the island I am inclined to think that the country people are averse to steady work, and have small respect for individual life or property. All this will have to suffer alteration under the new régime. The rural population will have to work to live, and the amount of the contributions they will be called upon to pay in the shape of taxation will assuredly be heavier than hitherto. Crime of all kinds will meet with speedy and severe punishment, and the people will have to learn and fully appreciate the fact that the justice meted out to them is no easy mistress to serve under.

"The transition stage while this lesson is being inculcated will, in all human probability, be productive of many elements of discontent, and the United States authorities must expect to encounter some unpleasant difficulties when dealing with these sources of mischief. In time the effect of just administration will solve the problem, but during the process of solution the Americans must not forget that they are dealing with a foreign race, alien alike in language, religion, and sentiment to the dominant features of their own great republic, and they will do well sometimes to call to mind the old Italian proverb of 'He who goes slowly goes far.'

"The population of Puerto Rico is of so mixed a character as to make it difficult to classify. Of the nine hundred thousand inhabitants of the island, fully one third are negroes, another third are mulattoes, and the remainder in many cases show marked traces of a mixture of African blood in their veins. Indeed, to draw a hard-and-fast line where the pure white families end and those with a trace of the negro begins, is almost impossible.

"The number of foreigners in the island is very limited. Of British subjects the total is stated not to exceed five hundred, including many negro immigrants from Jamaica and other West Indian colonies. France is more strongly represented, some two thousand persons claiming French citizenship, Ponce being their principal centre. In most of the chief towns Frenchmen are established in both wholesale and retail business, more especially in the latter branch of trade. The German colony, although not very numerous, has important interests both in financial matters and in the import and export trade of the island.

"The number of Americans resident in Puerto Rico before the war was very small, but here, as in Cuba, many of the natives have taken out naturalization papers in the United States for the purpose of claiming protection whenever they get into trouble. This abuse of the naturalization laws of the United States was not, however, carried on to the same extent by the Puerto Ricans as by the Cubans."

THE NEED OF GOOD ROADS.

Many questions reach the road inquiry bureau of the Agricultural Department respecting the character and conditions of the highways of Puerto Rico. In the absence of any great amount of detailed information on the subject, and as a general answer to inquiries, attention is called to the following extract of a letter from Brigadier General Roy Stone, who accompanied the army of invasion to the island. The communication was addressed to Mr. Martin Dodge, director of road inquiry, at the Omaha Exposition. General Stone says:

"I can only add to all that I have heretofore said in favour of the movement, a warning and reproof drawn from a country where, except for a few military lines, no roads have ever been built, and where the bulk of the product of a marvellously rich soil is carried to market on the heads of men and women or the backs of diminutive animals. As a result of this neglect, together with other kindred causes, the agricultural population of the island, although industrious and frugal, is so poor as to be almost without shelter, furniture, or clothing, and entirely without supplies of food, so that their trifling wages must be paid day by day to enable them to continue this hopeless existence.

APPENDIX. 273

"If the change to American possession can be made to bring the blessings of good roads to this island the lesson may react upon the continent itself and aid the work of road improvement at home; and this is one thing which encourages me in my local work here and consoles me for my absence from the greater field.

"With liberal treatment by our Government I hope to see here a quick example of the effects of good communications by road, railroad and water, on a heretofore homebound people."

Receipts and Expenditures of Puerto Rico from the Presupuestos General de Gastos é Ingresos for the Economic Year 1897-'98.

	Pesos.
Estimates for the Army	1,252,377.76
For Navy and Marine	222,668.26
Church and Justice	423,818.80
Public Works, etc	878,175.83
Hacienda (Realty)	260,800.00
General obligations	498,501.60
Total	3,536,342.19
Total receipts	3,939,500 00
Deficit	403,158.81

Of the appropriations, the estimates were:

For education	69,776.12
For the Church	193,610.00
As follows:	
Bishop of the diocese	9,000.00
Dean and archdeacon	5,500.00
Chantre (precentor)	2,500.00
Canons (*canonigos*)	10,000.00
Prebendaries (*racioneros*)	7,400.00
Endowment for ministers	6,000.00
Endowment of a chapel of music	4,000.00

	Pesos.
Parochial clergy (at 1,500 each)	16,500.00
Assistants (at 500 each)	12,000.00
Sacristans (at 150 each)	1,650.00
Curas of small parishes (at 1,000 each)	17,000.00
Assistant *curas* (at 600 each)	9,000.00
Sacristans (at 150 each)	2,500.00
Curas of small parishes (at 700 each)	40,000.00
Assistant *curas* (at 600 each)	9,600.00
Sacristans, at 150 each (*sin discuenta*)	8,700.00
Priest of Santo Domingo Church	480.00
Assistant priest of same	380.00
Sacristan in charge of the hermitage at Coamo	360.00
The congregation of missionaries	6,000.00
Total in salaries, etc	167,840.00
Total for "material"	26,270.00
Total, salaries and "material"	193,610.00

The Protocol of Peace under which Puerto Rico was Evacuated.

Protocol of agreement between the United States and Spain, embodying the terms of a basis for the establishment of peace between the two countries. Signed at Washington, August 12, 1898.

Protocol.

William R. Day, Secretary of State of the United States, and his Excellency, Jules Cambon, Ambassador Extraordinary and Plenipotentiary of the Republic of France at Washington, respectively, possessing for this purpose full authority from the Government of the United States and the Government of Spain, have concluded and signed the following articles, embodying the terms on which the two governments have agreed in respect to the matters hereinafter set forth, having in view the establishment of peace between the two countries, that is to say:

ARTICLE I.

Spain will relinquish all claim of sovereignty over and title to Cuba.

ARTICLE II.

Spain will cede to the United States the island of Puerto Rico and other islands now under Spanish sovereignty in the West Indies, and also an island in the Ladrones, to be selected by the United States.

ARTICLE III.

The United States will occupy and hold the city, bay, and harbour of Manila pending the conclusion of a treaty of peace, which shall determine the control, disposition, and government of the Philippines.

ARTICLE IV.

Spain will immediately evacuate Cuba, Puerto Rico, and other islands now under Spanish sovereignty in the West Indies, and to this end each government will, within ten days after the signing of this protocol, appoint commissioners, and the commissioners so appointed shall, within thirty days after the signing of this protocol, meet at Havana for the purpose of arranging and carrying out the details of the aforesaid evacuation of Cuba and the adjacent Spanish islands; and each government will, within ten days after the signing of this protocol, also appoint other commissioners, who shall, within thirty days after the signing of this protocol, meet at San Juan, in Puerto Rico, for the purpose of arranging and carrying out the details of the aforesaid evacuation of Puerto Rico and other islands now under Spanish sovereignty in the West Indies.

ARTICLE V.

The United States and Spain will each appoint not more than five commissioners to treat of peace, and the commissioners so appointed shall meet at Paris not later than October 1, 1898, and proceed to the negotiation and conclusion of a treaty of peace, which treaty shall be subject to ratification, according to the respective constitutional forms of the two countries.

ARTICLE VI.

Upon the conclusion and signing of this protocol, hostilities between the two countries shall be suspended, and notice to that effect shall be given as soon as possible by each government to the commanders of its military and naval forces.

Done at Washington, in duplicate, in English and in French, by the undersigned, who have hereunto set their hands and seals, the 12th day of August, 1898.

(Seal.)   WILLIAM R. DAY.
(Seal.)   JULES CAMBON.

INDEX.

Abercromby, General, 220.
Aborigines of Puerto Rico, 198 et seq.
Adjuntas, town of, 139.
Agouti, native mammal, 104.
Aguada, town of, 130, 139.
Aguadilla, port and town of, 9, 18, 130.
Agueynaba, Indian cacique, 210.
Alcalde, or mayor, 158, 234.
Allspice, how grown, 78.
Almuerzo, or breakfast, 193.
American flag, when raised, 232–234.
American troops, reception of, 225, 227; bravery of, 228, 229.
Añasco, town and river of, 140.
Anatto (Bixa orellana), 89.
Arecibo, port and town of, 9, 128, 129.
Armadillo, habits of the, 104, 105.
Arrowak Indians of Guiana, 200.
Arrow-root, cultivation of, 84.
Arroyo, port of, 10, 136.
Austin, Mr. O. P., on Puerto Rico, 259 et seq.
Aybonito, mountain town of, 140; United States troops at, 229.

Bamboo, uses of the, 93.
Banana, cultivation of the, 52, 54; production of, 244.

Banking and currency, 254.
Barceloneta, town of, 190.
Barranquitas, town of, 141.
Barros, hamlet of, 141.
Baskerville, Sir Thomas, 216, 218
Bayamon, town of, 141.
Beverages, some native, 186, 190.
Birds, species of, 109.
Black Hand, society of the, 230.
Bohio, or native hut, 51
Books on Puerto Rico (preface).
Bread-fruit, the, 94.
British attack on San Juan, 218.
British, the, capture Trinidad, 220.
Brooke, General, of United States army, 228, 230.
Buccaneers, or bucaneros, 219.
Bull-fighting, 184.
Bureau of American Republics, 243.

Cabinet woods, 92, 144.
Cable rates to the United States, 262.
Cabo Rojo, town of, 141.
Cacao, cultivation of, 67, 68, 245.
Caguas, town of, 141.
Camarones, or crayfish, 106.
Cambon, M., Ambassador of France, 274, 276.
Camuy, hamlet of, 142.

278 PUERTO RICO AND ITS RESOURCES.

Cangrejos, town of, 220.
Caparra, or Pueblo Viejo, 116, 209.
Carnicero, or butcher, 192.
Carolina, town of, 142.
Casa Blanca, Ponce de Leon's house, 121, 212.
Cassareep, a West Indian condiment, 84.
Cassava, a native plant, 83.
Castor bean, the, 88.
Cattle, statistics of, 259, 261.
Cavern of the dead, 151.
Caves and caverns, 129, 137, 144, 145, 150.
Cayey, hamlet of, 142.
Ceiba, hamlet of, 142.
Cereals, indigenous and exotic, 83.
Cervera, fleet of Admiral, 223.
Church, appropriations for the, 273, 274; the only Protestant, 262.
Ciales, town of, 142; massacres at, 230.
Cidra, hamlet of, 143.
Cigars, production of, 143.
Cimarron, animal run wild, 114.
Cinchona, cultivation of, 87.
Cinnamon, cultivation of, 80.
Citrus family, 75, 76.
Clergy, salaries of the, 273, 274.
Climate and climatic zones, 24, 30, 45.
Clove, cultivation of the, 80.
Coaling stations in the West Indies, 5.
Coamo, town and baths of, 143.
Coca, cultivation of the, 87.
Cocoa palm and products of the, 47, 50, 244.
Cockfighting and pits, 178, 184.
Coffee, exports of, 61; production of, in the island, 62, 243, 264; cultivation of, 63–66.
Columbus, voyages of, 97; traditions and accounts of, 130, 137.
Comeiro, town of, 143.
Commerce, statistics of, 254, 257.
Conquistadores, or conquerors, 198, 208.
Corozal, the town of, 143.
Cotton plant, the, 84.
Crabs, edible and scavenger, 106.
Culebra, island of, 22.
Currency, problems of the, 262.
Customs tariff (temporary), 249.

Day, Judge W. R., 274, 276.
Disease, causes of, 115.
Diseases, endemic, 114, 115.
Distances, table of, 157.
Dorado, town of, 143.
Drake, Sir Francis, 212-218.
Drinks, native, 188.
Drugs and dyes, 86.
Dye and cabinet woods, 86.

Earthquakes, phenomena of the, 30.
Eddoe, tropical food plant, 84.
Education, appropriations for, 261, 273.
Edwards, Bryan, historian, 200.
English in the West Indies, 212.
Estimates for 1897–'98, 273.
Evacuation of Puerto Rico, 232.
Exports and imports of the island, 255, 257, 264.

Fajardo, port and town of, 10, 20, 137.
Fibre-plants, 69.
Filibusteros, or filibusters, 219.

INDEX. 279

Fish of streams and coast, 106.
Fishing grounds, 107.
Fodder, common native, 191.
Folger, Captain, United States navy, 230.
Fruits of the island, 70, 265.

Game animals, 104.
Ginger, Jamaica, how raised, 81.
Gold, first taken to Europe, 95; where found in Puerto Rico, 100, 102, 245.
Gordon, Brigadier-General, United States army, 230, 232.
Government and captain-general, 158.
Guanica, port of, 10, 19, 224; landing United States troops at, 132.
Guayama, harbor and town of, 20, 136.
Guinea fowl run wild, 107.
Guira, native musical instrument, 185.
Gurabo, town of, 144.

Hanna, Consul, United States, advice from, 268.
Harbours of different coasts, 17–20.
Hatillo, town of, 144.
Hato Grande, town of, 144.
Hawkins, Sir John, 212, 216.
Henry, General, United States army, 228, 234.
Highways of the island, 152-156.
History of Puerto Rico, 208 et seq.
Hitchcock, Mr. F. H., on trade, 254 et seq.
Hormigueros, town of, 144.
Housekeeping, tropical, 192.
Humacao, town and port of, 10, 137.

Humming birds, 109.
Hurricanes, 28, 32–43.

Iguana, the, 105.
Immigrants, advice to, 268.
Imports and exports, 255, 264.
Indians of Puerto Rico, 198 et seq.
Indigo, 89.
Inland towns, 139 et seq.
Insect pests, etc., 112, 113.
Isabela, town of, 144.
Islands adjacent to Puerto Rico, 21, 23.

Jalap, where and how grown, 88.
Juana Diaz, town of, 144.
Juncos, town of, 144.

Kitchen, the Spanish, 193.

Lands, Crown, and other, 241, 246.
Lares, town of, 145.
Las Marias, town of, 145.
Loiza, hamlet of, 145.
Lechero, or milkman, 191.
Limes and lemons, 76.
Live stock, 259.
Logwood, 90, 91.
London Times, letter from the, 269.
Luquillo, the sierra of, 7; town and river of, 145.

Macias, Captain-General, 230, 231.
McKinley, President, 223.
Mahogany, tree and wood, 92.
Mails for Puerto Rico. See Postal Rates.
Maize, or Indian corn, 82, 85, 245.
Maloja, or corn fodder, 191.
Manati, town of, 146.

280   PUERTO RICO AND ITS RESOURCES.

Mango, fruit and tree, 71-73.
Mangrove, habitat and uses, 46.
Manioc, or cassava, 85.
Manufactures, 246.
Mariacao, town of, 146.
Mason, Prof. O. T., on Indians, 204.
Maunabo, the town of, 146.
Mayagüez, port, harbour, and valley of, 10, 18, 130.
Meals in the tropics, 193.
Miles, Major-General, United States army, 10, 132, 224, 227, 228.
Mineral and hot springs, 135, 142, 143, 144, 148.
Minerals of the island, 95, 245.
Mines and mining laws, 246.
Moco, town of, 146.
Mona, island of, 22.
Monito, island of, 22.
Montserrate, shrine of, 131.
Morovis, town of, 147.
Morro Castle, San Juan, 117.

Naguabo, port and town of, 10, 137.
Naranjito, town of, 147.
Navigation rules (1898), 252.
New Orleans, the United States cruiser, 230.
Nutmeg, history and cultivation of, 78, 80.

Orange, fruit and culture, 75, 244.

Palma christi, the, 88.
Palms, native and exotic, 51, 52.
Panadero, or baker, 192.
Parrots and pigeons, native, 81.
Patillas, town of, 147.
Peñuelas, town of, 147.

Pepper and vanilla, culture of, 81.
Perro monte, or wild dog, 114.
Piedras, town of, 147.
Pimento, culture of the, 77.
Pineapple, cultivation of the, 73, 74.
Plantain and banana, 53.
People, condition and character of, 159, 161, 164, 170-176; pastimes of the, 177, 184.
Playa of Ponce, 133.
Political divisions, 246.
Ponce, port and town of, 10, 133-136.
Ponce de Leon, first governor, 116, 125, 209, 211.
Population, density of, 160, 175.
Postal commissioners, 231; service and regulations, 231, 252 *et seq.*
Presupuestos (estimates) for 1897-'98, 273.
Priests, salaries of the, 274.
Products of Puerto Rico, 243 *et seq.*, 265.
Protocol of peace, the, 225, 274-276.
Provision grounds of natives, 94
Pueblo Viejo, town of Caparra, 209.
Puerto Rico, harbours of, 9, 10; latitude and location, 3-7; origin of the name, 130; physical features of, 7-9, 12; products of, 243 *et seq.*, 265; an American possession, 222.

Quebradillas, town of, 147.

Railroads of the island, 126, 127, 247 *et seq.*

INDEX. 281

Rainfall, table showing the, 258.
Rainy season, the, 25–27.
Reclus, M. Élisée, on Puerto Rico, 11.
Refresco, or refreshing drink, 188.
Rincón, hamlet of, 147.
Rio Grande, town of, 148.
Rio Piedras, town of, 148.
Rivers of Puerto Rico, 13–17.
Roads and highways, 152, 156, 272.

Sabana Grande, town of, 148.
Saint John, island of, 5.
Saint Thomas, island of, 5.
Salinas, town of, 136, 148.
Salt deposits, natural, 141, 149.
Sampson, Admiral, at San Juan, 221, 223.
San Germán, city of, 149.
San Juan, city of, 8, 9, 121–125; harbour and fortifications of, 17, 117–120; population of, 123; bombardment of, 120, 215, 218, 220.
San Sebastian, town of, 149.
Santa Cruz, island of, 5.
Santa Isabel, town of, 150.
San Turce, hamlet of, 150.
Santiago de Cuba, capture of, 220.
Sarsaparilla, culture of the, 89.
Schley, Rear-Admiral, United States navy, 230, 232.
Schomburgk, Sir R. H., 34.
Schools, appropriations for, 161.
Schwan, General, United States army, 228.
Seasons in Puerto Rico, information on the, 25–34.
Settlers, advice for, 239–242.
Shellfish, edible, 106.
Silk and silkworms, 91.

Snakes and serpents, 109–111.
Spaniards in Puerto Rico, 269.
Spices, soil and climate for, 77.
Steamers to and from Puerto Rico, 235.
Stone, Brigadier-General, United States army, 272.
Strategic base, Puerto Rico as a, 4, 6.
Sugar, cultivation of, 56, 58; amount of, exported and imported, 1, 61, 244.

Tea culture, possibilities of, 88.
Telegraph and cable lines, 126, 262.
Temperature, tables showing, 43, 258.
Territorial divisions, 158.
Toa Alta, town of, 150.
Toa Baja, hamlet of, 150.
Tobacco, cultivation of, 59, 60; export statistics, 61, 244.
Toledo, Don Federico, 219.
Towns of the interior, 139.
Trade of Puerto Rico with foreign ports, 236, 254, 264 et seq.
Transportation facilities, 247 et seq.
Trapiche de buey, or ox-mill, 55.
Trinidad, island of, taken by English, 220.
Tropical fruits, 265.
Trujillo Alto, town of, 150.
Turmeric, 90.

Utuado, town of, 150; cascade of, 150.

Valla de gallos, or cockpit, 178.
Vanilla and pepper, culture of, 81.
Vega Alta, town of, 151.

Vega Baja, town of, 151.
Vegetables of the tropics, 82.
Vieques, islands and products of, 21.
Vuelta Abajo, soils of the, 59.

Washerwoman, the West Indian, 195.
Wilson, General, United States army, 228.

Winter resort, Puerto Rico as a, 259, 267.

Yabucoa, town of, 137.
Yauco, town and port of, 132, 225.
Yunque, el (the Anvil), mountain of, 7.

Zabra, ancient Spanish vessel, 215, 217.

THE END.

D. APPLETON & CO.'S PUBLICATIONS.

WITH THE FATHERS. Studies in the History of the United States. By JOHN BACH MCMASTER, Professor of American History in the University of Pennsylvania, author of "The History of the People of the United States," etc. 8vo. Cloth, $1.50.

"The book is of great practical value, as many of the essays throw a broad light over living questions of the day. Prof. McMaster has a clear, simple style, that is delightful. His facts are gathered with great care, and admirably interwoven to impress the subject under discussion upon the mind of the reader."—*Chicago Inter-Ocean.*

"Prof. McMaster's essays possess in their diversity a breadth which covers most of the topics which are current as well as historical, and each is so scholarly in treatment and profound in judgment that the importance of their place in the library of political history can not be gainsaid."—*Washington Times.*

"Such works as this serve to elucidate history and make more attractive a study which an abstruse writer only makes perplexing. All through the studies there is a note of intense patriotism and a conviction of the sound sense of the American people which directs the government to a bright goal."—*Chicago Record.*

"A wide field is here covered, and it is covered in Prof. McMaster's own inimitable and fascinating style. . . . Can not but have a marked value as a work of reference upon several most important subjects."—*Boston Daily Advertiser.*

"There is much that is interesting in this little book, and it is full of solid chunks of political information."—*Buffalo Commercial.*

"Clear, penetrating, dispassionate, convincing. His language is what one should expect from the Professor of American History in the University of Pennsylvania. Prof. McMaster has proved before now that he can write history with the breath of life in it, and the present volume is new proof."—*Chicago Tribune.*

"Of great practical value. . . . Charming and instructive history."—*New Haven Leader.*

"An interesting and most instructive volume."—*Detroit Journal.*

"At once commends itself to the taste and judgment of all historical readers. His style charms the general reader with its open and frank ways, its courageous form of statement, its sparkling, crisp narrative and description, and its close and penetrating analysis of characters and events."—*Boston Courier.*

New York: D. APPLETON & CO., 72 Fifth Avenue.

D. APPLETON & CO.'S PUBLICATIONS.

THE BEGINNERS OF A NATION. A History of the Source and Rise of the Earliest English Settlements in America, with Special Reference to the Life and Character of the People. The first volume in A History of Life in the United States. By EDWARD EGGLESTON. Small 8vo. Cloth, gilt top, uncut, with Maps, $1.50.

"Few works on the period which it covers can compare with this in point of mere literary attractiveness, and we fancy that many to whom its scholarly value will not appeal will read the volume with interest and delight."—*New York Evening Post.*

"Written with a firm grasp of the theme, inspired by ample knowledge, and made attractive by a vigorous and resonant style, the book will receive much attention. It is a great theme the author has taken up, and he grasps it with the confidence of a master."—*New York Times.*

"Mr. Eggleston's 'Beginners' is unique. No similar historical study has, to our knowledge, ever been done in the same way. Mr. Eggleston is a reliable reporter of facts; but he is also an exceedingly keen critic. He writes history without the effort to merge the critic in the historian. His sense of humor is never dormant. He renders some of the dullest passages in colonial annals actually amusing by his witty treatment of them. He finds a laugh for his readers where most of his predecessors have found yawns. And with all this he does not sacrifice the dignity of history for an instant."— *Boston Saturday Evening Gazette.*

"The delightful style, the clear flow of the narrative, the philosophical tone, and the able analysis of men and events will commend Mr. Eggleston's work to earnest students."—*Philadelphia Public Ledger.*

"The work is worthy of careful reading, not only because of the author's ability as a literary artist, but because of his conspicuous proficiency in interpreting the causes of and changes in American life and character."—*Boston Journal.*

"It is noticeable that Mr. Eggleston has followed no beaten track, but has drawn his own conclusions as to the early period, and they differ from the generally received version not a little. The book is stimulating and will prove of great value to the student of history."—*Minneapolis Journal.*

"A very interesting as well as a valuable book. . . . A distinct advance upon most that has been written, particularly of the settlement of New England."—*Newark Advertiser.*

"One of the most important books of the year. It is a work of art as well as of historical science, and its distinctive purpose is to give an insight into the real life and character of people. . . . The author's style is charming, and the history is fully as interesting as a novel."—*Brooklyn Standard-Union.*

"The value of Mr. Eggleston's work is in that it is really a history of 'life,' not merely a record of events. . . . The comprehensive purpose of his volume has been excellently performed. The book is eminently readable."—*Philadelphia Times.*

New York: D. APPLETON & CO., 72 Fifth Avenue.

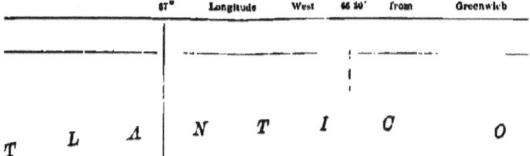

D. APPLETON AND COMPANY'S PUBLICATIONS.

OLLENDORFF'S METHOD OF LEARNING TO READ, WRITE, AND SPEAK THE SPANISH LANGUAGE. With an Appendix containing a Brief but Comprehensive Recapitulation of the Rules, as well as of all the Verbs, both Regular and Irregular, so as to render their Use Easy and Familiar to the Most Ordinary Capacity. Together with Practical Rules for the Spanish Pronunciation, and Models of Social and Commercial Correspondence. The whole designed for Young Learners and Persons who are their own Instructors. By M. VELÁZQUEZ and T. SIMONNÉ. 12mo. Cloth, $1.00. Key to Exercises in Method, 50 cents.

The superiority of Ollendorff's Method is now universally acknowledged. Divested of the abstractedness of grammar, it contains, however, all its elements; but it develops them so gradually, and in so simple a manner, as to render them intelligible to the most ordinary capacity. It is hardly possible to go through this book with any degree of application without becoming thoroughly conversant with the colloquial, idiomatic, and classic use of Spanish.

MERCANTILE DICTIONARY. A Complete Vocabulary of the Technicalities of Commercial Correspondence, Names of Articles of Trade, and Marine Terms in English, Spanish, and French; with Geographical Names, Business Letters, and Tables of the Abbreviations in Common Use in the Three Languages. By I. DE VEITELLE. 12mo. Cloth, $1.50.

An indispensable book for commercial correspondents. It contains a variety of names applied to various articles of trade in Cuba and South America, not found in other dictionaries.

A DICTIONARY OF THE SPANISH AND ENGLISH LANGUAGES. Containing the latest Scientific, Military, Commercial, Technical, and Nautical Terms. Based upon Velázquez's unabridged edition. 32mo. Cloth, $1.00.

This Dictionary, which is of a convenient size for the pocket, has proved very popular, and will be found an excellent lexicon for the traveler's handy reference.

THE MASTERY SERIES. Manual for Learning Spanish. By THOMAS PRENDERGAST, author of "The Mastery of Languages," "Handbook of the Mastery Series," etc. Third edition, revised and corrected. 12mo. Cloth, 45 cents.

The fundamental law of the Mastery Series is, that the memory shall never be overcharged, and economy of time and labor is secured by the exclusion of all that is superfluous and irrelevant.

D. APPLETON AND COMPANY, NEW YORK.

D. APPLETON AND COMPANY'S PUBLICATIONS.

THE COMBINED SPANISH METHOD. A New Practical and Theoretical System of Learning the Castilian Language, embracing the Most Advantageous Features of the Best Known Methods. With a Pronouncing Vocabulary containing all the Words used in the course of the Work, and References to the Lessons in which each one is explained, thus enabling any one to be his own Instructor. By ALBERTO DE TORNOS, A. M., formerly Director of Normal Schools in Spain, and Teacher of Spanish in the New York Mercantile Library, New York Evening High School, and the Polytechnic and Packer Institutes, Brooklyn. 12mo. Cloth, $1.25. Key to Combined Spanish Method, 75 cents.

The author has successfully combined the best in the various popular systems, discarding the theories which have failed, and produced a work which is eminently practical, logical, concise, and easily comprehended. The unprecedented sale which this book has had, and its steadily increasing popularity as a text-book, mark this as the leading Spanish method book now published.

THE SPANISH TEACHER AND COLLOQUIAL PHRASE BOOK. An Easy and Agreeable Method of Acquiring a Speaking Knowledge of the Spanish Language. By FRANCIS BUTLER, Teacher and Translator of Languages. New edition, revised and arranged according to the Rules of the Spanish Academy, by Herman Ritter. 18mo. Cloth, 50 cents.

The large sale and continued popularity of this work attest its merit.

THE SPANISH PHRASE BOOK; or, Key to Spanish Conversation. Containing the Chief Idioms of the Spanish Language, with the Conjugations of the Auxiliary and Regular Verbs. On the plan of the late Abbé Bossut. By E. M. DE BELEM, Teacher of Languages. 18mo. Cloth, 30 cents.

This little book contains nearly eight hundred sentences and dialogues on all common occurrences. It has been the aim of the compiler to insert nothing but what will really meet the ear of every one who visits Spain or associates with Spaniards.

A GRAMMAR OF THE SPANISH LANGUAGE. With a History of the Language and Practical Exercises. By M. SCHELE DE VERE, of the University of Virginia. 12mo. Cloth, $1.00.

This book is the result of many years' experience in teaching Spanish in the University of Virginia. It contains more of the etymology and history of the Spanish language than is usually contained in a grammar.

D. APPLETON AND COMPANY, NEW YORK.

D. APPLETON AND COMPANY'S PUBLICATIONS.

***SEOANE'S NEUMAN AND BARETTI SPAN-
ISH DICTIONARY.*** A Pronouncing Dictionary of the
Spanish and English Languages, with the addition of more
than 8,000 Words, Idioms, and Familiar Phrases. In Two
Parts: I, Spanish-English; II, English-Spanish. 1310 pages.
By MARIANO VELÁZQUEZ DE LA CADENA. Large 8vo. Cloth,
$5.00.

Velázquez's Dictionary, composed from the Spanish dictionaries of the Spanish Academy, Terreros, and Salvá, and from the English dictionaries of Webster, Worcester, and Walker, is universally recognized as the standard dictionary of the Spanish language. A unique and valuable feature of this dictionary is that it contains many Spanish words used only in those countries of America which were formerly dependencies of Spain.

***SEOANE'S NEUMAN AND BARETTI SPAN-
ISH DICTIONARY.*** Abridged by VELÁZQUEZ. A Dictionary of the Spanish and English Languages, abridged from the author's larger work. 847 pages. 12mo. Cloth, $1.50.

This abridgment of Velázquez's Spanish Dictionary will be found very serviceable for younger scholars, travelers, and men of business. It contains a great number of words belonging to articles of commerce and the natural productions of the Spanish-American republics, together with many idioms and provincialisms not to be found in any other work of this kind.

PRACTICAL METHOD TO LEARN SPANISH.
With a Vocabulary and Easy Exercises for Translation into English. By A. RAMOS DIAZ DE VILLEGAS. 12mo. Cloth, 50 cents.

This work is based upon the natural method of acquiring a knowledge of a language. The exercises are progressively arranged in parallel columns, English and Spanish, and present to the student a practical and simple method of learning the Spanish language.

SPANISH-AND-ENGLISH DICTIONARY. In
Two Parts. I, Spanish and English; II, English and Spanish.
By T. C. MEADOWS, M. A., of the University of Paris. 18mo.
Half roan, $2.00.

This Dictionary comprehends all the Spanish words, with their proper accents, and every noun with its gender.

D. APPLETON AND COMPANY, NEW YORK.

D. APPLETON AND COMPANY'S PUBLICATIONS.

LITERATURES OF THE WORLD. Edited by Edmund Gosse, Hon. M. A. of Trinity College, Cambridge.

A succession of attractive volumes dealing with the history of literature in each country. Each volume will contain about three hundred and fifty 12mo pages, and will treat an entire literature, giving a uniform impression of its development, history, and character, and of its relation to previous and to contemporary work.

Each, 12mo, cloth, $1.50.

NOW READY.

SPANISH LITERATURE. By James Fitz Maurice-Kelly, Member of the Spanish Academy.

"The introductory chapter has been written to remind readers that the great figures of the silver age—Seneca, Lucan, Martial, Quintilian—were Spaniards as well as Romans. It further aims at tracing the stream of literature from its Roman fount to the channels of the Gothic period; at defining the limits of Arabic and Hebrew influence on Spanish letters; at refuting the theory which assumes the existence of immemorial romances, and at explaining the interaction between Spanish on the one side and Provençal and French on the other. Spain's literature extends over some hundred and fifty years, from the accession of Carlos Quinto to the death of Felipe IV. This period has been treated, as it deserves, at greater length than any other."—*From the Preface.*

ITALIAN LITERATURE. By Richard Garnett, C. B., LL. D., Keeper of Printed Books in the British Museum.

ANCIENT GREEK LITERATURE. By Gilbert Murray, M. A., Professor of Greek in the University of Glasgow.

FRENCH LITERATURE. By Edward Dowden, D. C. L., LL. D., Professor of English Literature at the University of Dublin.

MODERN ENGLISH LITERATURE. By the Editor.

IN PREPARATION.

AMERICAN. By Prof. Moses Coit Tyler.

GERMAN.

HUNGARIAN. By Dr. Zoltán Beöthy, Professor of Hungarian Literature at the University of Budapest.

LATIN. By Dr. Arthur Woolgar Verrall, Fellow and Senior Tutor of Trinity College, Cambridge.

JAPANESE. By W. G. Aston, C. M. G., M. A., late Acting Secretary at the British Legation at Tokio.

MODERN SCANDINAVIAN. By Dr. Georg Brandes, of Copenhagen.

SANSCRIT. By A. A. Macdonell, M. A., Deputy Boden Professor of Sanscrit at the University of Oxford.

D. APPLETON AND COMPANY, NEW YORK.

D. APPLETON AND COMPANY'S PUBLICATIONS.

IN JOYFUL RUSSIA. By JOHN A. LOGAN, Jr. With 50 Illustrations in color and black and white. 12mo. Cloth, $3.50.

"Of extreme interest from beginning to end. Mr. Logan has animation of style, good spirits, a gift of agreeable and enlivening expression, and a certain charm which may be called companionableness. To travel, with him must have been a particular pleasure. He has sense of humor, a way of getting over rough places, and understanding of human nature. There is not a dull chapter in his book."—*New York Times.*

"Mr. Logan has written of the things which he saw with a fullness that leaves nothing to be desired for their comprehension; with an eye that was quick to perceive their novelty, their picturesqueness, their national significance, and with a mind not made up beforehand—frankly open to new impressions, alert in its perceptions, reasonable in its judgment, manly, independent, and, like its environments, filled with holiday enthusiasm."—*New York Mail and Express.*

"No more fresh, original, and convincing picture of the Russian people and Russian life has appeared. . . . The author has described picturesquely and in much detail whatever he has touched upon. . . . Few books of travel are at once so readable and so informing, and not many are so successfully illustrated; for the pictures tell a story of their own, while they also interpret to the eye a vivid narrative."—*Boston Herald.*

"A chronicle of impressions gathered during a brief and thoroughly enjoyed holiday by a man with eyes wide open and senses alert to see and hear new things. Thoroughly successful and well worth perusal. . . . There will be found within its pages plenty to instruct and entertain the reader."—*Brooklyn Eagle.*

"The book is a historical novelty; and nowadays a more valuable distinction can not be attached to a book. . . . No other book of travels of late years is so unalterably interesting."—*Boston Journal.*

"Mr. Logan's narrative is spirited in tone and color. . . . A volume that is entertaining and amusing, and not unworthy to be called instructive. The style is at all times lively and spirited, and full of good humor."—*Philadelphia Press.*

"Mr. Logan has a quick eye, a ready pen, a determination to make the most of opportunities, and his book is very interesting. . . . He has made a thoroughly readable book in which history and biography are brought in to give one a good general impression of affairs."—*Hartford Post.*

"Mr. Logan has presented in attractive language, reenforced by many beautiful photographs, a most entertaining narrative of his personal experiences, besides a dazzling panorama of the coronation ceremonies. . . . Read without prejudice on the subject of the Russian mode of government, the book is unusually able, instructive, and entertaining."—*Boston Globe.*

"Mr. Logan departs from the usual path, in telling in clear, simple, good style about the intimate life of the Russian people."—*Baltimore Sun.*

D. APPLETON AND COMPANY, NEW YORK.

D. APPLETON & CO.'S PUBLICATIONS.

GERMANY AND THE GERMANS. By WILLIAM HARBUTT DAWSON, author of "German Socialism and Ferdinand Lassalle," "Prince Bismarck and State Socialism," etc. 2 vols., 8vo. Cloth, $6.00.

"This excellent work—a literary monument of intelligent and conscientious labor—deals with every phase and aspect of state and political activity, public and private, in the Fatherland. . . . Teems with entertaining anecdotes and introspective *aperçus* of character."—*London Telegraph.*

"With Mr. Dawson's two volumes before him, the ordinary reader may well dispense with the perusal of previous authorities. . . . His work, on the whole, is comprehensive, conscientious, and eminently fair."—*London Chronicle.*

"Mr. Dawson has made a remarkably close and discriminating study of German life and institutions at the present day, and the results of his observations are set forth in a most interesting manner."—*Brooklyn Times.*

"There is scarcely any phase of German national life unnoticed in his comprehensive survey. . . . Mr. Dawson has endeavored to write from the view-point of a sincere yet candid well-wisher, of an unprejudiced observer, who, even when he is unable to approve, speaks his mind in soberness and kindness."—*New York Sun.*

"There is much in German character to admire; much in Germany's life and institutions from which Americans may learn. William Harbutt Dawson has succeeded in making this fact clearer, and his work will go far to help Americans and Germans to know each other better and to respect each other more. . . . It is a remarkable and a fascinating work."—*Chicago Evening Post.*

"One of the very best works on this subject which has been published up to date."—*New York Herald.*

A HISTORY OF GERMANY, from the Earliest Times to the Present Day. By BAYARD TAYLOR. With an Additional Chapter by MARIE HANSEN-TAYLOR. With Portrait and Maps. 12mo. Cloth, $1.50.

"There is, perhaps, no work of equal size in any language which gives a better view of the tortuous course of German history. Now that the story of a race is to be in good earnest a story of a nation as well, it begins, as every one, whether German or foreign, sees, to furnish unexpected and wonderful lessons. But these can only be understood in the light of the past. Taylor could end his work with the birth of the Empire, but the additional narrative merely foreshadows the events of the future. It may be that all the doings of the past ages on German soil are but the introduction of what is to come. That is certainly the thought which grows upon one as he peruses this volume."—*New York Tribune.*

"When one considers the confused, complicated, and sporadic elements of German history, it seems scarcely possible to present a clear, continuous narrative. Yet this is what Bayard Taylor did. He omitted no episode of importance, and yet managed to preserve a main line of connection from century to century throughout the narrative."—*Philadelphia Ledger.*

"A most excellent short history of Germany. . . . Mrs. Taylor has done well the work she reluctantly consented to undertake. Her story is not only clearly told, but told in a style that is quite consistent with that of the work which she completes. . . . As a matter of course the history excels in its literary style. Mr. Taylor could not have written an unentertaining book. This book arouses interest in its opening chapter and maintains it to the very end."—*New York Times.*

"Probably the best work of its kind adapted for school purposes that can be had in English."—*Boston Herald.*

New York: D. APPLETON & CO., 72 Fifth Avenue.

D. APPLETON AND COMPANY'S PUBLICATIONS.

H. *R. H. THE PRINCE OF WALES.* An Account of his Career, including his Birth, Education, Travels, Marriage and Home Life, and Philanthropic, Social, and Political Work. Illustrated. 8vo. Cloth, $3.50.

For the first time an accurate account of the life of the Prince of Wales is given in this entertaining and informing book. While there have been volumes dealing with special features of his life, a complete biography has not been published before. His social and philanthropic activities are described in this book, together with accounts of his visits to America, to India and the East, and his home life at Marlborough House and Sandringham. The numerous illustrations present a series of portraits from infancy to the present time, and also a remarkable collection of views of great ceremonial functions in which the Prince has taken part. On the historical as well as the personal side this biography offers peculiar attractions.

THE PRIVATE LIFE OF THE QUEEN. By a Member of the Royal Household. Illustrated. 12mo. Cloth, $1.50.

"The future historian will value 'The Private Life of the Queen' because it is in a sense so intimate. The contemporary reader will find it highly interesting for the same reason . . . The book is agreeably written, and is certain to interest a very wide circle of readers."—*Philadelphia Press.*

"A singularly attractive picture of Queen Victoria. . . . The interests and occupations that make up the Queen's day, and the functions of many of the members of her household, are described in a manner calculated to gratify the natural desire to know what goes on behind closed doors that very few of the world's dignitaries are privileged to pass."—*Boston Herald.*

THE LIFE OF HIS ROYAL HIGHNESS THE PRINCE CONSORT. By Sir THEODORE MARTIN. In five volumes, each with Portrait. 12mo. Cloth, $10.00.

"A full and impartial biography of a noble and enlightened prince. . . . Mr. Martin's work is not gossipy, not light, nor yet dull, guarded in its details of the domestic lives of Albert and Victoria, but sufficiently full and familiar to contribute much interesting information. . . . Will well repay a careful and earnest reading."—*Chicago Tribune.*

THE SOVEREIGNS AND COURTS OF EUROPE. The Home and Court Life and Characteristics of the Reigning Families. By "POLITIKOS." With many Portraits. 12mo. Cloth, $1.50.

"A remarkably able book. . . . A great deal of the inner history of Europe is to be found in the work, and it is illustrated by admirable portraits."—*The Athenæum.*

"The anonymous author of these sketches of the reigning sovereigns of Europe appears to have gathered a good deal of curious information about their private lives, manners, and customs, and has certainly in several instances had access to unusual sources. The result is a volume which furnishes views of the kings and queens concerned, far fuller and more intimate than can be found elsewhere."—*New York Tribune.*

D. APPLETON AND COMPANY, NEW YORK.

D. APPLETON AND COMPANY'S PUBLICATIONS.

NEW EDITION, REVISED TO MAY 1, 1898.

A HISTORY OF THE UNITED STATES NAVY, *from 1775 to 1898.* By EDGAR STANTON MACLAY, A. M. With Technical Revision by Lieutenant Roy C. Smith, U. S. N. New edition, revised and enlarged, with new chapters and several new illustrations. In two volumes. 8vo. Per vol., cloth, $3.50.

"When this work first appeared it was hailed with delight. . . . There are now important additions. The splendid material which Mr. Maclay has collected has been treated in admirable tone and temper. This history of the navy is a standard work."—*Boston Herald.*

"The new edition of this valuable book has rendered the general reader a service."—*New York Sun.*

"It will rank as a standard, and it will deserve the commendation it has had to the public."—*Chicago Tribune.*

"Few books of the kind have met with as cordial a reception as 'The History of the United States Navy,' by Edgar S. Maclay. . . . Since then the book has increased steadily in popularity, purely on its merits. The History shows how the navy was built up and its traditions kept alive as active forces through evil and good days. It shows how it has become possible for men to make a navy almost without ships. It shows more than that—the important fact that the United States to-day owes, if not its liberty, the full measure of its greatness to the navy primarily. . . . Maclay's 'History of the United States Navy' is the history of the importance of sea power to this nation."—*New York Press.*

"The author writes as one who has digged deep before he began to write at all. He thus appears as a master of his material. This book inspires immediate confidence as well as interest."—*New York Times.*

"Mr. Maclay is specially qualified for the work he has undertaken. Nine years has he devoted to the task. The result of his labors possesses not only readableness but authority. . . . Mr. Maclay's story may be truthfully characterized as a thrilling romance, which will interest every mind that is fed by tales of heroism, and will be read with patriotic pride by every true American."—*Chicago Evening Post.*

"It fills a place which has almost escaped the attention of historians. Mr. Maclay's work shows on every page the minute care with which he worked up his theme. His style is precise and clear, and without any pretense of rhetorical embellishment."—*New York Tribune.*

"It has been accepted as a standard authority, and its adoption as a text-book at Annapolis is a sufficient testimony of its technical merit."—*Philadelphia Press.*

"The author's clearness and compactness, and, where the action is important or animated, his spirited but never diffuse descriptive power, make the reading of his History a pleasure as well as a means of information on a subject of the highest interest to all Americans."—*Baltimore Sun.*

"The very best history of the United States navy in existence."—*Boston Journal.*

"The best history of the United States navy is that of Edgar S. Maclay."—*Philadelphia Inquirer.*

"Taken as a whole, this history of the navy is the best in print."—*New York Nation.*

"Every page thrills and gives fresh impetus to that yet unshaken faith that there is something in the republic that fashions her sons into invincible defenders of her flag and freedom."—*Boston Globe.*

D. APPLETON AND COMPANY, NEW YORK.

www.ingramcontent.com/pod-product-compliance
Lightning Source LLC
Chambersburg PA
CBHW030319240426
43673CB00040B/1217